Spread Betting the Forex Markets

An expert guide to making money spread betting the foreign exchange markets

D0231050

by David Jones

HARRIMAN HOUSE LTD

3A Penns Road
Petersfield
Hampshire
GU32 2EW
GREAT BRITAIN

Tel: +44 (0)1730 233870
Fax: +44 (0)1730 233880
Email: enquiries@harriman-house.com
Website: www.harriman-house.com

First published in Great Britain in 2010 by Harriman House.

978-1-906659-51-6

British Library Cataloguing in Publication Data
A CIP catalogue record for this book can be obtained from the British Library.

Printed in the UK by the MPG Books Group.

Contents

About the Author

David Jones started working in the City as a currency analyst after passing the Society of Technical Analysts diploma. He later moved into the spread betting industry where, most recently, he has been Chief Market Strategist at IG Index.

Part of his role in the industry has been providing market commentary and analysis to various media and he makes regular appearances in the mainstream press and on financial news channels such as the BBC and CNBC.

He has also been actively involved in client education. Over the years he has spoken to thousands of spread betting clients and has devised educational programmes on a wide range of subjects. This book was a natural development of that activity, drawing on his experience and his extensive knowledge in forex and technical analysis.

David would welcome any comments or questions about this book and can be contacted via email at forex@jonesdc.com.

Preface

What the book covers

First of all, this is not a book that explains the mechanics of spread betting in minute, mind-numbing detail. There is a brief overview of how spread betting works, but the various spread betting companies already do an excellent job in educating clients on the mechanics of this form of trading.

The book covers the basics of the foreign currency markets ("forex") and looks at what makes forex markets move. There is a detailed section on the important topic of risk management, and a brief overview of technical analysis from the perspective of studying forex markets.

The major part of the book presents some straightforward strategies for trading forex.

Who this book is for

The intended audience for this book are those who are interested in spread betting forex. But that is a very wide range of people with a wildly varying experience of trading.

Most of my own professional life within the industry has been spent educating those who are relatively new to spread betting, or those who may have been spread betting for some time but have not ventured away from their particular favoured market (e.g. shares). That is the sort of person I had in mind when writing the book.

I have endeavoured to make all sections of this book as accessible and useful to as many people as possible, regardless of previous experience. As I mentioned earlier, it is not designed to be an exhaustive introduction to spread betting, because there is more than enough information out there on that already. But if spread betting *is* completely new to you, the first chapter will, in my opinion, cover all you really need to know.

(If you are already making vast fortunes spread betting forex I would still hope there is the odd nugget for you in the book, and I hope it proves to be a useful and entertaining read for you in between dating supermodels.)

How the book is structured

When I sat down with the publishers to plan this book, it was straightforward enough to come up with logical sections that the book should be broken down into. I have based this on my experiences of talking to many clients over the years – there does seem to be a natural order to the questions on spread betting and forex so it seemed obvious that this book should follow that.

The first section is a recap on spread betting – just to make sure that we are all happy with the mechanics and terminology. Like a lot of things in life, spread betting is something that can sometimes be unnecessarily overcomplicated. I have tried to cut through the jargon and explain simply how it works (after all, it really is very straightforward).

The next section deals with the forex market itself. Like spread betting, this is something that can appear intimidating and complicated – but it really does not have to be. After reading this section you will be comfortable with various aspects of forex, such as what the quotes mean, what makes this market move, and why people trade it.

The following section is all about risk and how to manage it. By the end of this book I hope you are thoroughly fed up with me banging on about risk! If you are, I will consider it a job well done. This is the subject that we all give too little attention to in the beginning. However, it is absolutely critical, which is why there is a whole section on it. Managing risk sensibly helps us in so many different ways: it should ensure we do not get wiped out from a string of small losses, it helps us to figure out how much money we should be trading, and it should mean that trading is relatively low-stress.

The rest of the book looks at trading strategies. I have outlined some tried and tested approaches to forex trading with detailed examples of how they would have worked in real markets. I am a big fan of keeping things simple and these are the sorts of strategies that you should be able to put in practice for yourself straightaway.

Introduction

The purpose of this book is to get you started trading the forex markets using spread betting. These are both subjects that have really moved into the mainstream over recent years.

There are many reasons why forex continues to grow in popularity. I would argue that the huge size of the market makes it difficult for it to be affected much by single trades or a rogue piece of news. This can mean that trends in forex are more durable than those in many other markets – which is Good News for chartists. The size of the market also means the costs of trading are low.

And forex is seldom dull. On a quiet day in stock markets watching the short-term movements of many shares can be a mind-numbing experience. Whereas the often spectacular volatility in forex is what provides the opportunity for traders to make profits. Of course, it should be realised that this volatility does add additional risk – which is why there is a whole section on managing risk later in the book.

The final part of the equation has been the evolution of spread betting over recent years which, among many of its advantages, allows beginner traders to get involved in markets at a very low exposure (for example, trading at less than £1 per point). No longer do you need tens of thousands of pounds to dip your toes in the forex market.

Forex and spread betting are both subjects close to my heart. I've worked in and around the spread betting industry for the best part of the last ten years. I placed my first spread bet back in 1995, when the industry was very different to how it is today. My first proper job associated with finance was with a software company that supplied investment banks with real-time charting for the foreign exchange market. This is when I took the Society of Technical Analyst's exam and later went on to work as a forex technical analyst. It's fair to say that the vast majority of my approach to technical analysis and trading was learnt in the currency markets.

I've tried to bring all this experience together for this book and structure it so I can get across what I feel to be the important points to consider when spread betting the forex market.

There is a lot of rubbish out there about both of these topics. When Harriman House contacted me about this book, I was very keen to blow away some of the myths and misinformation. This book will explain the ins and outs of how to spread bet forex and give you some strategies to get you started trading.

I hope you enjoy reading it!

Part One

The Basics

Spread Betting

Spread betting has been around since the early 1970s, but it is the last ten years or so that has seen it really evolve and become, in my opinion, the best way for the vast majority of retail clients like me and you to trade financial markets.

It has grown in popularity for three reasons:

1. The advance of the internet and broadband has made it possible to provide real-time data direct to your desktop – wherever you are. Spread betting companies were amongst the first financial companies to offer online trading platforms and additional tools such as charting, stop losses, etc.

2. The dot com bubble and, of course, the subsequent bursting of this bubble at the beginning of this century, and then the financial crisis sparked off by sub-prime loans, has pushed financial markets onto the front pages. This has made people more aware of some of the wild gyrations seen in financial markets and perhaps more sceptical about the talents of professional financial managers. This in turn has led many people to want to take more control of their own investments, and also to see if they can profit from some of this shorter-term volatility.

3. And finally, as the spread betting industry has grown and competition has increased, the spreads have been driven down very sharply, which has meant it has evolved into a very cost-effective way of trading.

But to the new spread betting client, it can still look confusing and may be a bit daunting at first glance, so let's clear that up before we get into some of the other topics.

The spread bet price

Let's get one thing out of the way from the start. Spread betting companies do not predict where the price is going to go. There is no crystal ball hidden from public view at the back of the dealing room. The spread bet price you see is the market price, with usually a bit added on either side of the bid and the offer. It may be worth at this point taking a step back because, to some people, the notion of a 'two way price' is somewhat confusing.

If you check the daily paper and look at, for example, the price of Vodafone, it may show that it closed at 120p – so you think the price of Vodafone is 120p. However, there is more to it than that. If you called your stock broker you would discover there are actually two prices for Vodafone: a price if you are selling and a price if you are buying. So the broker may quote you 119.9p/120.1p, meaning:

- you can *sell* Vodafone shares at 119.9p, or

- you can *buy* Vodafone shares at 120.1p.

This is called the *bid/offer spread*. All markets have a spread – and spread betting is no different.

So let's get back to the topic of the book, the forex market.

Assume we are looking at the price of the British pound against the US dollar; the spread bet price will depend on where the forex market is trading at that particular time. The bid/offer quote may be something like this: 1.6300/1.6303. If you are buying, then you pay the higher price and if you are selling your trade gets done at the lower price.

At least once a month a customer will ask me why can't he buy at the lower price and sell at the higher price. The quick answer to this is that spread betting companies are not charities! The spread represents – as it does in all financial markets – the profit for the institution acting as market maker (in this case the spread betting company). Market makers take on the risk of providing prices across a range of markets and their reward for taking this risk is the spread.

So, the spread bet price will move around as the underlying market moves.

Figure 1.1: Twelve hour chart of GBP/USD daily spread bet contract

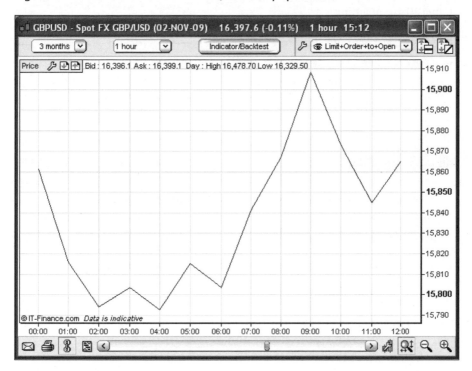

Figure 1.1 shows how the price of the spread bet will change as the underlying market moves around. This chart represents the first 12 hours of trading on 28 September 2009. The market is GBP/USD – the British pound/US dollar exchange rate. All the spread bet does is move up and down as the exchange rate changes; it is just mimicking the moves in the forex market of this particular currency pair.

Another thing worth clearing up (if you haven't figured it out already) is that spread betting is not a market on its own. Many people seem to think that there is a whole new set of rules that need to be learnt when trading using spread betting. There really isn't. Spread betting is not a more complicated product, unlike products such as options or covered warrants where factors such as volatility, time to expiry and strike prices need to be taken into account.

Spread betting is transparent

A reason for the appeal of spread betting is the *transparency* of the prices. Spread betting is simply the mechanism you use to carry out your trade. This transparency has increased vastly in recent years with the introduction of the *daily* spread bet contract [more on this later]. All of the analysis is applied to the underlying market, because all the spread bet price does ultimately is mirror this.

> ### Key point:
>
> All markets have a two way price – the bid and the offer. Spread bet companies do not forecast where a market is going to go, the spread bet price moves up and down as the underlying market moves.

Time frames for trading

This is a very important topic (and one we will cover in more detail when we look at trading strategies) but it is worth a quick mention right here at the beginning.

Probably the most common mistaken assumption about spread betting – and trading in general – is that it has to be very short term. You have to be in front of your screen before eight in the morning when UK markets swing into action, right through till nine at night when the US shuts up shop.

Let's take this one step further.

Forex is a true 24-hour market so surely you should be in front of your screen in the wee small hours, coffee in hand, just keeping an eye on what is happening in the Asian session?

And isn't trading all about clicking "buy" and "sell" all day long, jumping in and out for a few points profit (hopefully) every time?

You don't need to be stuck to your screen

Don't get me wrong, if I ran a spread betting company I would love it if all the clients traded this way, because every time they trade they are paying spread, which is a little bit of profit for me – thanks very much. But the reality is for most of us as clients we don't have the time to sit there and watch every tiny change in price around the clock. I am sure there are people out there who make money from scalping the markets in this way, but it is not the only way.

Personally, I think markets are easier (I would never say *easy*) to predict over the medium term (days/weeks/months) than over the very short term (seconds and minutes).

I think one of the things that puts people off trading is that they think they do not have the time. But you do not need to be tied to a screen, watching prices for all your waking hours.

Let's look at an example from the real world that we should all be familiar with.

Say you thought the UK stock market index, the FTSE 100, was going to rise from 4500 to 5000 over the next two weeks. You decide to buy. Now, if you sit there and watch it around the clock for the next two weeks is it going to go up any faster? Of course it isn't. So by using tools, such as stop losses, you can place your trade, place an order to manage your risk and then get on with something far more productive away from the screen.

The point I am making here is that trading does not have to be just about day trading. Trading this way is a baptism of fire for anyone who is new to the markets. And it is something that many who have been involved with markets for some time (again, me included) have very little interest in.

We will be examining some slightly more relaxed approaches to trading in the strategies part of this book.

Key point:

Spread betting, and trading in general, does not necessarily have to be about the very short term. You do not have to be glued to the markets for hours at a time to trade forex.

Trading in terms of pounds per point

As I said earlier, spread betting just reflects what is going on in the underlying markets – whether that is a share price, a stock market index, a commodity or a currency pair.

The main thing you need to get your head around when it comes to understanding how spread betting works (and this should hopefully only take you a few minutes to grasp) is that you trade in terms of *pounds per point*. This is the same across all markets that you trade using spread betting, it is particularly relevant when trading forex, as changes in price in these markets are traditionally quoted in points (or pips) anyway.

So the first thing to understand is: what is a one point movement in the market in question?

Again, let's start with an example we are all hopefully familiar with, the FTSE 100 index. If this goes from 4000 to 4100, that is a one hundred point move. So going back to spread betting, if you had bought, say, £2 per point at 4000 then sold when the FTSE hit 4100, then the market has

> Some charting packages – including the one I use – do not show the decimal place when showing forex. While this can take some getting used to because, for example, 1.6100 gets represented as 16,100, it is one of those things that you do not notice after a short while.

moved 100 points in your favour, you have traded £2 per point, therefore it represents a £200 profit on this particular trade.

When it comes to forex markets, the way the currency pair is quoted can vary slightly from one spread bet company to the next, but one-point moves in popular currency pairs are as follows.

GBP/USD (British pound/US dollar)

Traditionally quoted to four decimal places, a GBP/USD price would look something like this: 1.6100. This example price means a pound is worth one dollar and 61 cents. If the market were to move up by one point the quote would then be 1.6101.

The following chart shows July to early August 2009 for GBP/USD where the price moved from 1.6050 on 8 July to as high as 1.7000 by 5 August. This is a 950 point move (1.7000 – 1.6050).

Figure 1.2: GBP/USD

EUR/USD (euro/US dollar)

Like GBP/USD, this pair is also traditionally quoted to four decimal places, so a typical price looks something like this: 1.4100. Again, if EUR/USD moves down, for example, to 1.4000 then that is a 100 point move.

The following chart shows EUR/USD from the end of July 2009 to the first week of August. It has moved from 1.4000 on 29 July to 1.4430 by 5 August – a move of 430 points.

Figure 1.3: EUR/USD

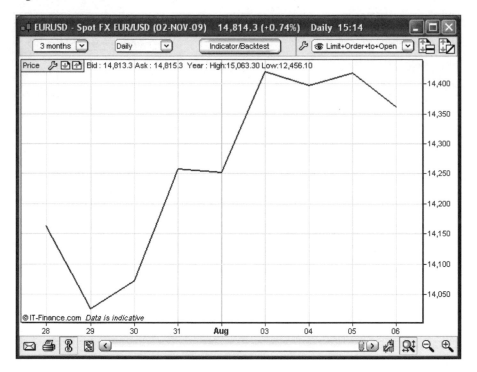

USD/JPY (US dollar/Japanese yen)

The market convention for this one is to quote it to two decimal places, for example, 95.00. If USD/JPY were to rise by 50 points, the quote would become 95.50.

The following chart shows USD/JPY from August to early September 2009. USD/JPY peaks at 97.60 on 7 August and finishes up at 92.35 at the end of the chart, 3 September. This chart therefore represents a fall of 525 points.

Figure 1.4: USD/JPY

If you are not sure what a one point move is for the particular currency pair you are following, do not be afraid to contact your spread bet company. It is a source of constant bafflement to me how some people will let confusion over little things like this put them off placing a trade – when the answer can be explained in a matter of seconds. There are more important things to worry about when trading!

We will be coming back to this idea of point movements time and again when we get into the fundamentals of how forex works and look at some trading strategies.

Key point:

When spread betting you are trading in terms of pounds per point, which makes it easier to calculate your potential risk and profit on a trade, and size your trade accordingly.

The different contracts available and margin trading

If we wind the clock back ten years, the only spread betting contracts available were similar to the futures markets. So if you wanted to trade GBP/USD and it was currently May, you could have a choice of trading a GBP/USD June contract, a September contract and maybe even a December contract.

This would be the first point of confusion: did this mean you were locked into your trade until the expiry of the contract, regardless of what happens? No – you can trade out whenever you want to (assuming the market is open of course). If you bought GBP/USD September and changed your mind ten seconds later, you could sell out to close your position.

The second confusing thing about the various contracts available would be the prices quoted. They would all be slightly different, and would also normally be different from where GBP/USD was trading in the cash market. Many new to this form of trading would take this as meaning that the spread betting company was skewing its price to reflect where it thought GBP/USD was going to be trading at some point in the future. This is not the case – as I mentioned earlier, spread betting companies are not in the business of forecasting where a market is going.

So why the difference in price for these different contracts?

Margin trading

With spread betting, you are trading on margin. This means you do not need to tie up the full value of your trade – just a portion of your overall total trade value. In effect, a smaller sum of money controls a much bigger financial position.

An example is the quickest way to explain this. We'll look at how it works for shares first and then currencies.

Forgetting about spread betting for a moment, let's say you wanted to buy 1000 shares of, say, BT which was currently trading at 100p. If you were going to buy actual shares then usually you would need the £1000 in your stock broking account, plus of course a little bit more to cover stamp duty and commission.

Using spread betting, you could have the same exposure to BT Group by buying BT at £10 per point. Your total position is £1000 (£10 per point x 100p entry price). But you do not need to have £1000 in your account to do this trade. With spread betting, and other products that trade on margin, you only need to have the initial margin deposit as specified by your spread betting company (and of course any additional funds to cover any potential running losses). So if we assume that the initial margin requirement for BT Group is 10%, then in this example all we would tie up on our account is £100. That £100 controls the £1000 overall position. This is the whole principle of trading on margin – a small sum of money controls a much bigger overall position.

Margin trading the forex markets

When it comes to trading forex, most spread bet companies don't express that margin required as a percentage of your overall exposure, but as a multiple of the amount you are buying or selling per point. Let's assume your spread betting company's margin requirement for GBP/USD is quoted as "300 times stake". This means that if you buy £1 per point when GBP/USD is trading at, for example, 1.6000, then the margin required for this trade is £300 (£1 per point x 300 deposit requirement).

If you are interested in how big your actual position is, when trading £1 per point at 1.6000, this is easily calculated. The "per point" part of the trade refers to the fourth decimal place of the GBP/USD price. So when calculating the overall size of the trade, we forget the decimal place. The size of your overall position is £1 x 16000 (entry point) which translates into a £16,000 position in GBP/USD. So, once again, a small amount of money is controlling a much bigger financial position; in this example a £300 initial deposit has allowed us to open a £16,000 trade on GBP/USD.

This is how it works for all markets in spread betting, with varying deposit amounts from one market to another, set by the spread betting company and normally dependant on factors such as volatility for that market and the liquidity available.

You can see that by trading on margin, the spread betting company is effectively letting us borrow a significant part of the value of the trade. But as we all know, there is no such thing as free money and this is why you will see the slightly different values of the future contracts for the various future expiries. Because we are, in effect, borrowing money from the spread betting company to trade, there is an interest charge built into the price, reflecting the cost of carry for that trade into the future. Apart from the spread, which is of course present in all markets, this finance charge is the only compulsory cost of spread betting.

The daily contract

What really changed spread betting over recent years was the introduction of the daily spread bet contract. This is a spread bet that *technically* expires at the end of every day, so there is no cost of financing built into the price. This is always the contract that more closely reflects the prevailing price in the underlying market (the *cash price,* or *spot price* as it is often referred to, particularly in the forex market).

Although strictly speaking these daily contracts expire at the end of the day, in practice the majority of clients choose to have them *rolled over* into the next day (assuming their trade is still open, i.e. it hasn't been stopped out or manually closed by the client).

It is when the trade is rolled over that a financing charge is made. This can be a source of confusion to the new spread betting client, so let's look at how it works.

Spread betting companies usually express the financing cost as LIBOR, plus a percentage. LIBOR stands for London Inter Bank Offered Rate and is a widely used financial markets interest rate. If we assume your spread betting company charges LIBOR plus 2.5% for financing, and LIBOR is currently 3%, then the cost of financing is 5.5% (3% LIBOR + 2.5% the additional cost). This is an *annual* charge, so the pro-rata daily amount using these numbers would be 0.015% (5.5% / 365).

Let's look at how that works in practice for a couple of small trades on daily contracts.

FTSE 100 example

In the first example let's use another popular market, the FTSE 100. Our trader buys £2 per point when the FTSE is at 4000, trading the daily contract. The total exposure, or size of the position, is £8000 (£2 per point x 4000 entry point). The trade is still open at the end of the day and the market is still at 4000. The spread betting company rolls the position over into the next day, applying the financing charge. Based on the numbers in the previous paragraph, a charge of 0.015% will be applied, which comes out at £1.20 (£8000 total position size x 0.015%).

GBP/USD example

Let's now apply it to our forex trade on GBP/USD. In the earlier example, we bought £1 per point of GBP/USD at 1.6000. Assuming a daily contract was used, the trade gets rolled into the next day so financing applies. This would be £2.40 (£16,000 total position size x 0.015%). Any profit or loss achieved on that day gets realised and credited or debited into the client's account.

So in both these examples there would be a financing charge for every day the trade was left running if the trade was done using a daily contract.

Financing charges not a significant cost

While the above numbers are for illustration purposes only, and it can vary slightly from one company to another how financing gets calculated and applied, it can be seen that in the great scheme of things, while it is a cost to trading, it is not a significant one. The charges are equivalent, with interest rates so low in 2009, to barely a couple of points or so every day – this really is a drop in the ocean when we are dealing with markets that regularly move in excess of 100 points a day.

Of course, financing is still a real cost to trading on margin so, although it may be negligible on a day-to-day basis for short-term traders, it could end up being a sizeable amount for a long-term trade. This is why products such as spread betting that use margin are particularly suitable for what I would call medium-term trades (two to three months or less). You can, of course, run a trade for as long as you want but you need to bear in mind that even if the market does not move much in that time, there is still the financing aspect to take into account.

At the time of writing this book, interest rates around the world were at record low levels, so this has become an even smaller cost than usual when spread betting. I have seen many people get bogged down in worrying about the financing aspect, but there are bigger things to concern ourselves with when it comes to trading. When you actually start trading, I don't think you will give a second thought to it because we are talking about such small sums in comparison to the typical movements in forex markets.

Key point:

There are usually different contract expiries available when spread betting. Typically, the daily (or rolling) contract price does not include a financing cost – this will be applied separately. Other contracts will usually have the financing cost built into the price. This is why different contracts will have different prices – it is not the spread betting company forecasting a market is going to rise or fall.

Example of a trade

Let's walk though an example of a trade, just to demonstrate how all this ties together.

- We'll stick with **GBP/USD** and a **daily contract.**

- We will assume we have told our spread betting company we want the contract to be **rolled over** at the end of the day (assuming we are still in the trade). With some spread bet companies the default setting for your account is to roll over all contracts automatically. With other companies you need to let them know this is what you want to happen – but usually you only need to tell them once.

- We will assume the **deposit requirement** by the spread betting company is 300 x stake and that our account balance is currently £1000, with no other trades open.

Okay, we're ready to go.

Placing the trade

We bring up the dealing ticket and the price is shown as 1.6000/1.6003. We have decided to buy, and the size we are going to trade is £1 per point. We input the appropriate information on the dealing ticket and click buy. The trade is executed and we buy £1 per point GBP/USD on a daily contract at 1.6003.

We now have £300 of our account tied up against this trade as initial margin. This leaves us £700 available for other trades (although of course we would be well advised to leave some of this spare to cover any potential running losses on this trade).

As the day goes on, GBP/USD edges higher. By the close of the day it is trading at 1.6053/1.6056.

Rollover at close

We have already set up daily contracts to be rolled over via the trading platform.

So what happens now at the close?

The trade will be automatically rolled over into the next day. This is done by effectively closing out the position and opening a new one (this is all done for us automatically by the spread betting company).

As we saw above, the GBP/USD contract is 1.6053 to sell (we bought earlier in the day at 1.6003). So this profit of 50 points is realised – which translates into a £50 profit because we bought £1 per point. This £50 is credited to the balance of our spread betting account.

Because we are rolling the trade over, finance is due. There are assumptions to make here and I am going to assume the financing charge is LIBOR + 2.5%, with LIBOR currently at 3%. So the daily finance cost is around 0.015%. Our exposure at the close is £1 x 16053 = £16,053. So the amount due as finance would be approximately £2.41 (£16,053 position size x 0.0015% financing charge).

The term "close" is a bit of a misnomer of course as the forex market is a 24-hour one. But spread betting companies need to choose an arbitrary time when the contract expires or rolls over. This can vary from one company to another, but for the purposes of this example we will assume the spread betting company chooses 8 p.m. UK time as its notional close for the forex markets.

This £2.41 finance charge will be applied in a slightly different way depending on which spread betting company we are trading with.

1. One way it will be applied is as a straightforward debit from our account, which we will see on the daily statement. This is usually applied at the time the spread betting company chooses as their 'close' for forex. So, in this example, all of this will happen at 8 p.m. We will then be in the trade at £1 per point from the new level of 1.6053, where the position was rolled over.

2. Alternatively there may not be a debit from the account, but the trade will be opened for the next day at an adjusted level to reflect the financing charge. We know the financing is £2.41 and this trade has been done at £1 per point. So to express the financing in points terms, £2.41/£1 equates to 2.41 points. The position would be closed at 1.6053 and then immediately re-opened at 1.6055.41 (1.6053+2.41).

However your spread betting company does it, the net result is still the same – financing has been charged and the trade is still open.

Of course, don't forget that the trade can be closed out whenever desired (assuming the market is open). In this example all we would need to do is to sell £1 per point to realise our profit or loss and close the position. We could get out of this trade ten seconds after we got in if required – I used an example of a position running overnight to highlight how rolling over a daily contract works.

It is a surprisingly long-winded process to explain!

In practice, placing the trade is a matter of seconds and the rollovers will happen automatically. But I think it was worth walking through it to explain the process because I have found many new spread bet clients will end up tying their brain in knots worrying about how things like margin and rollovers work, and the costs of finance, when there are much more important things to be exerting our mental energy on.

Spread betting summary

Let's summarise what we have covered so far:

1. Spread betting is a very efficient way of trading a wide range of financial markets – and is particularly well suited to forex.

2. With spread betting you trade in terms of pounds per point. A concept we will come back to time and again when looking at strategies.

3. Apart from the bid/offer spread (which is present in all markets) the only other charges for spread betting, because you are trading on margin, are the financing costs associated with this. This applies to both running a daily spread bet contract overnight, or trading on one of the quarterly contracts. With daily contracts, this financing charge is applied every day the trade is open. With quarterly contracts the costs of financing for the trade is reflected in the price quoted.

   Importantly, while the financing aspect is a cost to trading, in the great scheme of things it is a negligible one for most short to medium term trades as you will have experienced when you have placed your first few trades.

As this book is about spread betting forex, it is time to look at this particular financial market in more detail.

Forex Explained

We have looked at the ins and outs of using spread betting to trade and why it has become so popular with traders over recent years. We will now take a look at what the forex market is all about.

Background of the forex market

Unlike most other financial markets, this market has no physical location and no central exchange. It operates 'over the counter' through a global network of banks, brokers, corporations and individuals. The forex market is the world's largest financial market, operating 24 hours a day, with enormous amounts of money traded on a daily basis. While it can be difficult to put an exact figure on the amount traded on a daily basis, the latest Bank for International Settlements estimate puts it at $3.98 trillion.[1] In one day, every day.

Forex originally developed to aid international trade conducted in different currencies by various organisations – whether they were governments, companies or individuals. While these markets primarily existed to provide for the international movement and exchange of money, it was not too long before it drew the attention of speculators. Today, an enormous percentage of forex market activity is driven by speculation and arbitrage – such that currencies are traded today like any other commodity.

The forex market, as we know it today, was effectively born on 15 August 1971, when President Nixon took the USA off the gold standard. This meant that any perceived value of the US dollar was no longer underpinned by the equivalent amount of gold. It created the notion of unpegged, or floating, currency exchange rates. The growth of the internet over the past decade or so has meant that now it is possible for individual traders to trade a massive range of currency pairs from almost anywhere in the world.

---

[1] To put $3.98tr in some context, that's five times greater than the annual budget of the UK government.

What is a currency pair?

Currencies are not quoted in isolation; if someone says, "the last three months have seen the pound strengthen," then this is only half the story. It can only have strengthened relative to another currency, for example, the US dollar, or the Japanese yen, or the euro, or maybe even all of them.

One currency is always quoted against, or in relation to, another. Hence we have a wide range of markets such as British pound/US dollar (GBP/USD), US dollar/Japanese yen (USD/JPY), euro/Swiss franc (EUR/CHF), and so the list goes on.

It is common shorthand in the forex market to refer to the various currencies, and the different currency pairs, by three letter codes: So the US dollar is USD; the British pound is GBP; euro is EUR; Japanese yen is JPY.[2]

Currency nicknames

As we all know, financial markets love their jargon and some currencies have their own nicknames. Probably the most widely used and best known is the one for GBP/USD – this is often referred to as 'Cable', recalling the days when exchange rate transactions for this pair were wired between London and New York via a transatlantic cable. Possibly the best known one after Cable is 'the Loonie' – the Canadian dollar, as the coin bears the image of the common loon, a Canadian bird. Don't worry too much about the nicknames – I would stick to the proper names to avoid any potential confusion.

---

[2]For further information on currency codes see:

en.wikipedia.org/wiki/Currency_codes

The most traded currencies

In theory, any currency can be traded against that of another country, but in practice most of the volume in the global forex markets is concentrated in just a few currencies (as can be seen in the following table).

Rank	Currency	Code	% Daily Share, April 2007
1	United States dollar	USD	86.3%
2	Euro	EUR	37.0%
3.	Japanese yen	JPY	17.0%
4	Pound sterling	GBP	15.0%
5	Swiss franc	CHF	6.8%
6	Australian dollar	AUD	6.7%
7	Canadian dollar	CAD	4.2%
=8	Swedish Krona	SEK	2.8%
=8	Hong Kong dollar	HKD	2.8%
10	Norwegian krone	NOK	1.9%

Source: Bank for International Settlements Triennial Central Bank Survey, December 2007

As I mentioned, whilst in theory you can trade a whole variety of exotic currency pairs, it is clear that the vast majority of trades involve the US dollar against another currency. When starting to look at forex I would not worry too much about going outside the major pairs to start with. While there are no hard and fast rules confirming which pairs are actually the 'majors', hopefully the following list should not provoke too much disagreement:

EUR/USD   (euro/US dollar)

USD/JPY   (US dollar/Japanese yen)

GBP/USD   (British pound/US dollar)

USD/CHF   (US dollar/Swiss franc)

USD/AUD   (US dollar/Australian dollar)

USD/CAD   (US dollar/Canadian dollar)

There should be more than enough going on in these markets, regardless of your chosen time frame, to keep you busy.

Quoting conventions and terminology

The first quoted currency is referred to as the *base currency*, and the second is sometimes referred to as the *term currency*. So, with the British pound/US dollar exchange rate (GBP/USD), the pound is the base currency and the US dollar is the term currency.

What does the currency quote actually mean, if we see, for example, GBP/USD currently quoted as 1.6800? It tells you that one British pound will buy one US dollar and 68 cents. This is the same for all pairs, so if:

- USD/JPY is trading at 95.00 then a US dollar buys 95 Japanese yen.

- EUR/GBP is at 0.9550 then a euro buys 95 and a half pence.

Do you need to remember this jargon?

No, the main point you need to appreciate is that when you, for example:

- **buy** GBP/USD, you are speculating that the pound will *rise* against the US dollar, and

- **sell** USD/JPY, you are speculating that the US dollar will *fall* versus the Japanese yen.

GBP/USD or USD/GBP?

It is appropriate to mention the correct way for quoting a currency pair. There is not really a right or wrong way, but there is a traditional way of doing this which you should follow to avoid confusion.

For example, when talking about the exchange rate between the UK and USA you *could* express it as how many US dollars one pound will buy (GBP/USD), or how many pounds one US dollar will buy (USD/GBP). Both will give different results of course, although both are strictly correct. But the market convention is to quote it as GBP/USD. This is equally true for all the other possible currency pairs – although they can be quoted in either order, there is a market convention when it comes to trading.

> ### Key point:
>
> The thing you need to understand is when you click buy or sell for a currency pair, you are buying or selling the base, or first quoted, currency versus the second.

Strength and weakness in forex

On the basis that a picture paints a thousand words, let's look at a chart of GBP/USD from July 2008 to July 2009.

Figure 2.1: GBP/USD July 2008 to July 2009

We can see that in the summer of 2008, GBP/USD was trading around 2.0000 – a pound would buy you a couple of dollars. But, by January of 2009, the price had fallen towards 1.3500 – one British pound was buying only one US dollar and 35 cents. This was a slide in excess of 30% – a significant drop in forex terms.

But a source of confusion for some is what actually weakened – was it the pound or the US dollar?

Going back a few paragraphs, the pound in this chart is the first quoted currency, so if the chart is going *up* we are seeing GBP *strength* (and correspondingly US dollar weakness). In the first part of the chart, we have seen a drop in GBP/USD so what we are looking at is weakness in the pound – and correspondingly strength in the US dollar.

The second half of the chart shows GBP/USD recovering some of the losses. The currency pair moves from the 1.3500 area in January up towards 1.6500 by June. We are now seeing strength in the pound versus the US dollar. If we had bought GBP/USD in January and held through this rise, it would have represented a profit – we would have been speculating that the pound was going to rise versus the US dollar and would have been proved right.

Key point:

Forex is a market made up of currencies that are quoted in pairs – it is a two-dimensional product. The various currencies do not move in isolation; if one currency is said to have risen, it is in relation to another currency that has weakened. When you are buying or selling, it is the first quoted currency that your trade is based on: if you buy, for example, GBP/USD you are speculating that this exchange rate is going to go up (pound strength/dollar weakness); if you sell, for example, EUR/JPY you are speculating that this particular exchange rate is going to go down (euro weakness/Japanese yen strength).

What moves the forex market?

The short answer to this is: potentially everything.

[Well, that was a short answer! However...]

The novice to forex trading wants to know what economic figures should be watched to figure out how the market is going to move. Is it unemployment, interest rates, inflation, political changes, consumer sentiment, corporate profits, GDP figures? Yes, to all of them. And all the other stuff I haven't mentioned. All will have had an effect on the forex markets at one time or another.

A reflection of confidence

A high level way of looking at forex is as a reflection of the confidence investors and traders have in one part of the world in relation to the other. For example, if the US economy is expected to weaken at a much faster rate than the European zone, you would expect EUR/USD to rise as speculators see the euro as the better bet out of the two. It is a fair assumption to view the longer-term trends in various currency pairs as a barometer of the overall market sentiment to one economic zone versus another.

There is seldom just one set of economic data that moves currency pairs. If that was the case it would all be too simple and a particular exchange rate would very quickly move to whatever level everyone agreed was fair value based on that particular economic fact. In practice a whole host of factors will come into play.

One relatively recent example of this was the introduction of the euro to world forex markets in 1999 (it would still be three years before notes and coins were introduced into the Eurozone, but from 1999 it was actively traded against a host of other currencies). And it was not well received...

Figure 2.2: EUR/USD 1999 to 2001

To say the euro was unloved by forex markets in the first couple of years of its trading life would be an understatement – it became something of a one-way bet. It dropped from 1.1700 in January 1999 to as low as 0.8250 in October 2000; a drop of 3450 points or a loss in value of nearly 30% against the US dollar.

As already explained there is seldom only one reason behind the movements in currency pairs and the euro is a case in point. There were various fundamental factors all adding up to that all-important ingredient: market confidence.

There really was quite a disconnect between the two world economies following the dot com bubble bursting. Growth and business confidence in the USA was still strong, whereas in the Eurozone, in countries such as Germany and France, the outlook remained downbeat. Because the US looked like the more attractive proposition, there was an outflow of capital from Europe and people were buying US dollars. So simple supply and demand played its part. Plus, for the euro there was the political dimension: it represented a single currency, a single central bank and an arguably single economic policy for what many viewed as widely different economies in the Eurozone. Political leaders of countries outside of the euro would occasionally not hide their scepticism of the grand project. And this did nothing for sentiment. The economic and political fundamentals of the first couple of years of the Euro's life in the forex market all added up to a lack of credibility, which translated into negative sentiment demonstrated by the chart above.

This recent historical example hopefully goes some way to explain what a jigsaw the forex market can be when it comes to the driving factors behind the various fluctuations. Ultimately, as I wrote at the beginning, forex is a reflection of market confidence in one economy versus another – but there are many ingredients that go into the mix that will influence this.

One of these is interest rates. Let's take a look at how these influence the forex market.

The effect of interest rates on currencies

According to the Bank of England:

> the impact of interest rates on the exchange rate is, unfortunately, seldom that predictable.[3]

So, as illustrated in that quote, this is a difficult topic and as such I don't want you to think you are about to read the final word on how interest rates affect forex. However, in the following section we're going to look at the major points that a forex trader needs to know.

---

[3] www.bankofengland.co.uk/monetarypolicy/how.htm

I will use fictional interest rates to highlight the theory. Let's assume the UK interest rate you can borrow money at is 2%, the US rate for money on deposit is 8%, and finally the GBP/USD exchange rate is 1.5000. Let us also assume that the exchange rate is going to stay static for a year (a ridiculous assumption but just suspend your disbelief for a little longer).

There is clearly a no-brainer transaction here: to borrow pounds at 2%, convert to dollars and receive 8% interest in the USA. In a year's time you can change back to GBP at the same rate and you have made a risk-free 6%. If you have heard the term 'carry trade' this is the sort of transaction it refers to – borrowing a currency where the interest rate is low and buying a currency (or indeed other assets such as shares) where the interest rate, or perceived return, is higher.

Of course, in the real world this situation is not a zero risk one, because exchange rates fluctuate and markets can move quickly to eliminate anomalies like the fictional one I have outlined. But it does demonstrate that interest rates can affect the attractiveness or otherwise of one country's currency versus another – but seldom in the clear-cut way I dreamt up.

It's not black and white

Unfortunately, interest rates rarely lend themselves to simple analysis. For example, interest rates may be high to combat rampant inflation. So while high interest rates could make a currency attractive, rampant inflation usually would not (as that might mean that the central bank of that country will start printing more cash – devaluing the currency).

I haven't written this with the intention of deliberately confusing you, but to illustrate that there is very rarely a simple answer to how important various fundamental factors are to forex markets and in which direction they will cause the market to move – particularly in the short to medium term, which is the main focus of this book.

Markets can be slaves to fashion

Fashion is possibly too flippant a word to use here, but the perceived importance of various economic factors can vary from one period to the next. At one point inflation data can be the all-important economic release everyone is waiting for, and then six months later it could be unemployment numbers that keep forex traders watching the screen.

Recent history demonstrates how the importance of economic data can change with time. We will follow the fortunes of the GBP/USD rate from late 2007 to 2009.

Figure 2.3: GBP/USD 2007–2009

At the end of 2007, GBP/USD had been out to its highest levels in 26 years against a backdrop of US dollar weakness against many major currencies and a relatively positive outlook for the UK economy versus the US one.

2007, you may recall, was when the wider world first became familiar with the phrase 'sub-prime'. The UK had the Northern Rock crisis but it is probably fair to say that it was still believed to be more of a US problem at that stage. The UK economic fundamentals, whilst not the best they had been, did not look that shaky and the UK looked poised to ride out any storm at least as well, if not better, than most of the developed world.

So 2008 started off as a fairly boring one for GBP/USD with the currency pair bouncing around the 2.0000 level.

But it can be seen that the last five months of the year were anything but boring: with GBP/USD dropping relentlessly from August through to December.

Did the market care about interest rates and/or inflation?

To an extent, yes – but it is safe to say it was not at the forefront of traders' minds. This was the eye of the financial storm when the shares of what were considered blue-chip UK banks (such as HBOS, RBS, Barclays and Lloyds) fell by extraordinary amounts.

It was a financial meltdown that saw even the likes of Lehman Brothers disappear down the plug-hole. In the face of this, who was really bothered about whether inflation was a point up or down from the previous period? It was all about security and confidence – and the UK did not look like a safe bet. Supply and demand. Lots of sellers of GBP pushed it lower as investors and traders saw the US dollar as a safer haven.

Figure 2.4: GBP/USD January 2009

And then the situation went from bad to catastrophic in January of 2009.

In the space of a couple of weeks, GBP/USD dropped by around 10% – back to levels not seen since the mid-1980s. Lack of confidence still played its part here as the financial sector remained under pressure, and the bailouts of the banks by the UK government also weighed heavily on sentiment. Just how much extra debt was the UK taking on to prop up the banks, who was going to pay for this, and as the financial sector comprised such a major part of the UK economy, would UK plc be on its knees for years?

Only 12 months previously many viewed the UK as well-placed to weather the storm, and yet now there were many who felt that it would end up being the country that struggled the most with the global downturn.

There were many fundamental factors in play here. There was the stability and profitability (or lack of it) of a major part of the UK economy – the banking sector. Then there was the issue of the amount of government debt and how that debt would be reduced in the future. Then there was the recovery from recession question: what would the UK Gross Domestic Product look like in six months time? And, of course, the situation showed no signs of improving soon, so that raised the prospect of increased unemployment.

No single factor

This section was all about what drives forex markets. Hopefully I have demonstrated that my quick answer at the beginning – everything! – was not just a flippant one. A variety of economic fundamentals will affect forex – and their importance will vary at different points of the economic cycle. Ultimately they all come together and are reflected back at us as a view of market sentiment, which is best demonstrated by the longer-term trends seen in exchange rates.

It is precisely this combination of significant economic fundamentals that can make forex such a fascinating market to be involved in. Unlike individual shares, currencies aren't moved around by 'micro' news such as profit warnings, director buying or anything as humdrum as quarterly profits. As currencies are such huge, international instruments there is the opinion (which I would subscribe to) that trends in these markets are more robust and take more to change than those in other assets – a fact that has not gone unnoticed, of course, by technical analysts (and this is the approach that will be explored when we later look at trading strategies).

Even though the fundamental focus can change, there are certain market announcements that are still closely followed – I will wrap up this section by highlighting what I think are the big ones to keep an eye on.

Key monthly announcements

As forex is a 24-hour global market it is impossible to expect anyone to stay abreast of every iota of economic news that could have an effect, as and when it comes out. As a general rule of thumb, it tends to be the big announcements that hold the focus of forex traders month in and out – that is, those to do with unemployment and interest rates.

The biggest of these is the monthly **US Non-Farm Payrolls** report (the American unemployment statistics) – typically released on the first Friday of the month at 13:30 UK time (it will very occasionally be held on the second Friday of the month).

Many spread betting platforms now have economic calendars as part of their service so it is very easy to keep aware of what announcements are coming up over the next few days. Financial websites such as Bloomberg are also a good way of seeing exactly what the market is looking for from the announcement – because it is how much the actual number varies from what the market was expecting that will cause the forex market to move around, rather than the absolute number itself.

One final point on this; some traders have the opinion that you should not hold a trade through an economic announcement – you should close it out before the announcement is made. While I think this could be a possible approach for very short-term traders, if you are taking a medium to longer-term approach to trades then you should not be overly concerned about the (normally) short-term burst of volatility after an announcement is made. As mentioned before, there are so many economic announcements that can affect the forex market, trying to get out ahead of each one (and then back in after the announcement has happened) is a pointless exercise.

It could be that the announcement ends up being a complete shock and the market reverses direction from the one you were trading – that's what stop losses are for. The flip-side of this is that you could also end up with a surprise move in your favour.

The only exception I would make to trading over a major news event would be if you do not have a trade on just before an announcement is due. Let's assume there are 15 minutes to go until the US announces its latest interest rate policy. You do not have a trade on. Bearing in mind in 15 minutes time the market could be plus or minus 100 points or more from where it is now, surely it is better to wait and let the dust settle and look at the market in question once the announcement is out of the way.

The mechanics of trading forex

There are three main ways we can get access to the forex markets:

1. futures

2. margined forex accounts

3. spread betting

This book is focussed on spread betting, but it won't do any harm to look at some of the alternative ways we can trade forex.

1. Futures

Traditionally, forex was the realm of major financial institutions. Whilst private investors could get involved directly in the markets, it was only open to those with significant amounts of capital to risk. So for many years private investors would have to look at currency futures as the main route to trading forex. These are still available today and trade on the Chicago Mercantile Exchange (CME). Volumes traded are in the region of $100 billion a day – a sizeable amount by any standard, but of course still dwarfed by the interbank forex market.

With the advent of other ways for the private investor to trade forex, I struggle to see the benefits of using currency futures for most people. This isn't because I work in the spread betting industry – I used to use currency futures a lot back in the mid-1990s. But with futures you trade in terms of fixed contract sizes. You buy or short-sell x number of contracts (e.g. the GBP/USD contract is $6.25 per point). Many new entrants to forex want to try their hand at a smaller size, at least to start with, and there is just not the flexibility to do this with futures.

Plus, of course, the futures are based on the underlying interbank markets, so why not just trade that in the first place?

2. Margined forex accounts

In addition to futures, there is the standard type of margined forex account that has become available over the past ten years or so – many of the spread bet companies will also provide these types of account. There is a slight variation in how these accounts will operate, depending on who you trade with, but the principle is the same – you are trading the forex market on margin, in a way not too dissimilar to spread betting.

They tend to operate as something of a mishmash between trading the futures way and trading in the interbank spot market. You can buy or sell the various currency pairs using contracts, which again tend to have fixed sizes reflecting the size of the position. Many of these accounts do offer mini-contracts, which are typically for $10,000 exposure to the chosen currency pair.

It is a perfectly good way of trading forex but, like futures, you can lose a degree of flexibility when it comes to choosing the size of your trade. Unlike futures, however, the prices normally reflect the underlying exchange rate trading in the spot market. For most people outside the UK, this form of margin trading has become the default way of trading forex over recent years.

In the UK we have yet another alternative to all of these – and that is, of course, spread betting.

3. Spread betting

We have already covered spread betting in the first section. Like currency futures and margined forex accounts, spread betting uses leverage so you only have to put up a small portion of the overall position as an initial deposit. In addition, spread betting is a tax-free way of trading, unlike other methods which are normally subject to capital gains tax.

You do always have to bear in mind that tax laws can be changed, and will probably be different for you if you are not a UK resident, but historically, and at the point of writing this book, no tax is due on profits from spread betting for UK taxpayers. Of course, you don't have it both ways: any spread betting losses cannot be offset against other capital gains.

I mentioned earlier that I thought spread betting was the ideal way to trade forex. One of the reasons for that is all down to the idea of trading in pounds per point. As we already know, when we talk about moves in forex markets we talk about point, or pip, moves – and this is the same for spread betting.

So when using spread betting for trading forex it is very easy to quickly calculate your potential risk. For example, if I am going to trade GBP/USD, buying at 1.6100 with a stop loss at 1.6000 (100 points away), and I only want to risk losing £200, then I know I need to trade £2 per point (£200 risk on trade, divided by 100 points, the distance away I am going to place my stop loss).

Also, many spread bet companies now let you trade in fractions of £1 per point. If, on the above trade, I only wanted to risk losing £150, then I need to buy £1.50 per point. This makes it very easy to tailor the size of my trade to fit my overall risk profile; something that is not so easy when you are forced to trade in fixed contract sizes, like in the futures markets.

> ### Key point:
>
> There are a variety of products available to us for trading forex, each slightly different. Because of the developments in the industry over recent years I think spread betting has become arguably the simplest and most efficient way.

The final points to cover, now we have dealt with the nuts and bolts of the forex market, is why it has always been a high volume market, and why it has become so popular with private traders around the world over recent years.

Why forex has become such a popular market

Big and liquid are probably the best ways to describe the world's forex market, meaning that this is a playing field that should be level for all participants. The sheer volume of business seen in forex means it is nigh on impossible for any one trader or institution to bully the market, and it is usually easier to get big trades filled in forex than any other market.

In this section we're going to quickly look at four factors that make forex markets attractive to trade:

1. a true 24-hour market

2. very low bid/offer spreads

3. trending-ness

4. volatility

1. A true 24-hour market

There is another aspect to liquidity and that is the availability of the forex market on a time basis, allowing you to respond to developments: it is always open during the week. This can be advantageous regardless of what time frame you plan on trading. Whether it is intra-day, jumping in and out for a few points, or as an end of day trader looking to catch a bigger move over days and weeks.

For instance, no matter where you live and what time zone you operate in, you can trade online during the Asian, London or New York sessions. The forex markets move 24 hours a day. The global foreign exchange market opens early on Monday mornings in New Zealand (night-time Sunday, UK time). It is usually very liquid 24 hours a day, all the way to the New York close around 5 p.m. on Friday (around 10 p.m. UK time).

Some people may not initially see a 24-hour market as such an attraction; they may feel happier with something like the London Stock Exchange that shuts up shop at 4:30 p.m. But think about that for a second – even though the LSE has a definite close, does that mean that there is nothing going on later that affects share prices? Of course there is. The US market, arguably the most important stock market in the world, is open for a further four and a half hours. The movements here will have an impact on UK shares, it is just that we will have to wait till 8:00 a.m. the next day to see them (which may result in gapping as prices open significantly above or below their previous close). With forex we have a fluid market open around the clock that can react to world events as they happen. The sensible use of orders (such as stop losses) can control our trades for us around the clock – without the need to watch screens 24 hours.

2. Very low bid/offer spreads

The cost of doing business is also another reason for the appeal. Over the years the forex bid/offer spreads have grown more competitive and advantageous for individual traders. Today, you can buy and sell any of the major currencies with a spread of just a few points – paying the same sort of bid/offer spread as the major institutions.

I can remember when the spread betting spread on many of the major currency pairs was well in excess of ten points! Competition and increased popularity has driven the spreads down, which makes it arguably one of the most cost-effective markets out there to trade.

Let's look at this in a bit more detail and compare the cost of trading a popular UK share, Vodafone, with GBP/USD. The following table shows the comparative bid/offer prices at one time on 5 October 2009.

Instrument	Bid	Offer	Spread	Spread as % of Bid	Previous week's range (points)	Spread as % of 1 week range
Vodafone	138.71	139.04	0.33	0.24%	7.2	4.6%
GBP/USD	1.5940	1.5943	3	0.02%	356	0.84%

This shows a few things (not least what a boring share Vodafone can be!)

It demonstrates the low cost of doing business in the forex market. I have chosen to take the spread as a percentage of the bid price to highlight what the percentage spread is of the total trade size. Of course, the Vodafone spread is a very tight one – a third of a penny – but it is still ten times bigger in percentage terms than the corresponding spread in GBP/USD.

But for me the most important information is in the final column. Tight spreads are all well and good, but if a market does not move much it can still eat into your overall potential on the trade. But you can see that there is more than a fivefold difference in the respective volatilities of the two markets in relation to the spread.

Key point:

Put simply, your cost of doing business in forex, when looking at the spread as a percentage of your position size, or when expressed as a percentage of the sort of volatility that can be expected, is much lower than even very liquid markets such as Vodafone.

3. Trending-ness

The idea of trending-ness (which, OK, I doubt is actually a real word) sums up another quality that makes this market appealing to traders of all sorts of different time frames. And that is the tendency of forex markets to demonstrate more sustainable trends (in both directions of course) than other markets.

This was something I touched on when looking at what drives forex markets. Because they are the most heavily traded of all financial instruments, it usually takes a lot to provoke a significant change in their long-term direction. A good comparison (which I can't claim as my own) is thinking of an individual share price as a speed boat which can chop and change direction with relative agility, while a forex pair is an oil tanker which requires a big turning circle and plenty of time to change direction (unless it is sinking, of course, but I think the comparison starts to break down there so we can ignore that aspect...)

It is obvious to see why forex is considered a more trending market than others; as previously mentioned it is driven by major economic factors, and the sheer volume seen in these markets means that no single trade is ever really going to have that big an effect. So any minor blip in an existing trend still requires a reasonable shift in the underlying fundamentals – and, of course, correspondingly a shift in sentiment among many market participants.

4. Volatility

Another reason for the appeal of forex is volatility.

Forex markets are seldom dull. Even when there is not much going on and there is no major news flow for traders to focus on, it is not unusual for forex markets to move in the region of 50 to 100 points a day. And when these markets do pick up they can really move. To make money, most traders need a market to do something other than flatline, so this volatility makes forex attractive.

Of course the savvy trader recognises that hand-in-hand with additional volatility goes additional risk. If this element of the forex market is ignored, then the trader will no doubt find out very quickly why risk should be the number one consideration before clicking buy or sell.

So, before we start to consider potential trading strategies, we are going to take a long, hard look at the subject of risk.

Managing Risk

So far in this book we have covered the nuts and bolts of spread betting and what the forex market actually is. You should now understand the basic principles of these two subjects.

So surely that's it – right?

Let's have a look at some trading strategies and we can get on with our domination of the global currency markets...

Nothing could be further from the truth.

Putting it bluntly: everything covered so far is irrelevant unless the idea of risk, risk versus reward, and risk management is understood and applied. The lack of appreciation of just how big a part this four letter word plays in trading is ultimately the biggest reason why trading any market can turn into a painful (and expensive) baptism of fire for so many.

For the purposes of this section we can break risk down into three areas.

The three components of risk

First of all there is the *risk of being wrong* on any one individual trade.

This is the reality that unfortunately, regardless of how invincible we think our strategy may be, it is not going to be right all the time. We need to have something in place that gets us out if things go wrong, so we live to trade another day. If a trader doesn't have a mechanism for doing this, and instead is determined to hang on in there until the trade comes good, he or she will very probably have a short lifespan in the market.

I think the idea of having a stop loss in place – an order to close the trade at a loss if it gets to a certain level – is appreciated by most people when they start trading. But occasionally this is not adhered to, or let slip:

"just this one time"

because, of course (and here comes the most expensive phrase in investing or trading):

"this time it's different..."

The placing and use of stop losses is one thing that needs to be considered when we are addressing the subject of risk. Every sensible trading strategy needs to consider how the trade will be exited if things don't go to plan. A strategy that does not have some sort of rule to get out if things don't pan out as first thought is not a strategy at all.

Then there is the second part of our risk jigsaw: the *risk versus reward* consideration of any one trade.

Put bluntly, this is the part that should ask:

> *"Is the potential reward of this trade really worth what my loss will be if it doesn't work out as planned?"*

I think this is an area ignored by many people and they end up entering trades virtually blind. If the risk versus reward is wrong you could end up with a strategy that is right nine times out of ten, and still loses you money. You would be surprised what a common experience this is for many people.

Last, but definitely not least, the final area where we need to consider risk, and I am convinced this is absolutely critical, is *position sizing*. This deals with how much to risk on any one trade, relative to the size of your overall trading pot.

Far too many of us when first setting off on trading spend too long worrying about things such as:

> *What markets should I trade?*
>
> *What account shall I open?*
>
> *Should I use moving averages or stochastics?*
>
> *Should I hold my trade for a few seconds or run it for a few days?*

Trust me, all of this stuff is irrelevant unless your position sizing is sorted out. As this is the most important aspect of risk management, let's deal with it straightaway.

Position sizing

Much has been written on this over the years, and much of that has been ignored by traders (to their cost) – and I can assure you I speak from experience.

My early experience

When I first started trading, using futures in the mid-1990s, I started off with a £5000 account. Because of the way futures contracts work, you have fixed contract sizes for a fixed size per point, which on many contracts back then started from $10 per one point move. Of course with spread betting now you can trade at a much, much lower level than this – but it wasn't the case for me back then.

So, with my shiny new futures trading account, and all the confidence and invincibility of the freshly qualified chartist, I started off on what I imagined would be my Soros-like journey through the financial markets. I was confident that it would be just a matter of time before central banks cowered at the sound of my name, as I unerringly rode the highs and lows of the world's currencies.

I was looking for reasonably big moves, over a few days at least, and my stop losses were in the region of at least 100 to 200 points away from where I got in. Forget about the strategies I was using at the time, or what markets I was trading, or how many hours a day I was glued to the screen. As mentioned before, all of that is irrelevant if your position sizing is wrong.

Let's just look at the simple financial facts of what I was doing.

An impressive ignorance of risk

I was trading contracts that were typically around $10 per point. I was risking, let's say on average, 150 points per trade (determined by how far away my stops were from my entry levels). That translates into $1500 risk per contract (I was only trading single contracts).

So, I was risking losing (if my genius analysis actually turned out to be wrong) about £1000 per trade.

The maths at this point is not difficult.

I started off with £5000 in my account. My typical loss, if a trade went wrong, was around £1000. I was risking losing 20% of my account on any one trade. Let's fast forward a few months from when my account was opened. Did I:

1. achieve total domination of the largest financial market in the world, or

2. have five losing trades on the trot at some point and effectively blow up my account?

I will leave you to figure that one out.

I think this is the biggest mistake, bar none, that we all make when starting out: risking far too big a percentage of our account on any one trade. Whether the account in question is just £500, or £5 million, is irrelevant; it is all down to the proportion of the amount risked.

Greed, of course, plays a big part here. The reason that so many are drawn to trading is the appeal of potentially large profits from correspondingly big moves. I am sure this has played a part in drawing so many individuals into forex over recent years. But of course there is no such thing as free money (have I mentioned that before?) and risk goes hand-in-hand with reward. For the novice, however, the risk part of this equation is rarely given as much consideration as the reward side of it.

Overconfidence

I also believe that when we start trading we have probably spent at least some time doing research. We may have read some books, trawled the internet or attended a seminar. So we feel we have a bit more knowledge than the average new trader to financial markets.

Many of us, when we first start, are overconfident in our ability to predict the markets and the subject of risk is not given too much consideration. It is all too easy to look at some recent big moves up or down in your chosen forex market and think:

"How hard can this really be – it was obvious it was going to do that..."

It is part of human nature to think we are the exception to the rule, but this can be a very expensive attitude when it comes to risk.

However, I am sure that enough of you will have read those last few paragraphs and still be thinking:

"Fair enough, but that applies to everyone else. I am a special case."

This is a very dangerous attitude.

It is, of course, entirely up to you, and if you are anything like I was back then, you may well end up ignoring what I say and risk the majority of your account on one 'can't lose' trade right from the off. It's a free country. Good luck to you and I hope you enjoyed your exciting, but brief, foray into trading. For others: let's get into it.

The mechanics of position sizing

If position sizing is so incredibly important where should we start?

The thing that you need to figure out is what percentage of your trading pot you are willing to risk on any one trade.

Most sensible approaches to position sizing suggest that you should be looking at risking somewhere between 1% to 3% of your overall trading pot on any particular trade. Whenever I mention this at seminars, I can see some people's shoulders slump:

> *"This seems so small, it is going to take me ages to get my orange Lamborghini if I am trading in this way."*

This is true, but the saving grace of this approach is it ensures that you are still in the game after a losing streak. And we will have streaks where we just can't seem to get it right (the biggest one I personally had in 2009 was six losers on the trot). It happens. In the same way that you will have runs when you can seem to do no wrong and the market seems to respond perfectly to your every buy or sell.

So if you accept that no system is going to be right all the time, and if you also accept that occasionally you are going to have a bad run, then it seems to be common sense that you need to have some form of protection from blowing your account up.

But it most definitely does *not* mean that you should go around placing, for example, a 1% stop loss on every trade. This is the other extreme that we will come to when we start examining stop-losses in more detail. The position sizing consideration should come before you even start looking for trades.

As usual, the easiest way of illustrating this is via an example.

Example

Let's assume our trader has decided he has total risk capital of £5000 for trading. The decision then is what percentage of the trading pot he is willing to risk on any one trade. After giving this some thought the trader decides to risk 3%. So what this means is that if any trade goes wrong, it is only going to lose £150 (£5000 trading pot x 3%). Of course as the trading pot increases/decreases then the amount risked on each trade, if we are sticking to the 3% rule, will fluctuate.

But starting off with £5000 in the account, £150 is the figure the trader is willing to risk losing on any one trade. Let's say a trade is identified: our trader thinks that GBP/USD is going to increase from 1.6000 and, from analysing his charts, decided that a sensible place for a stop loss is 1.5925. This is 75 points away from the entry level (1.6000 - 1.5925 = 75).

It has already been decided that if any trade goes wrong it is only going to lose £150.

So, on this particular trade, our trader knows he should trade £2 per point. If it goes wrong, and the trade gets stopped out for a loss, then that will be £150 (75 point loss x £2 per point). A perfectly manageable risk based on the size of the account.

Trade summary – calculation of position size

Variable	Value
Trading pot	£5000
Trading risk per trade	3% (£150)
Trade entry price	1.6000
Stop loss level	1.5925
Stop distance	75 pts (1.6000 - 1.5925)
Trade size per point	£2 (£150 / 75)

Let's jump forward and assume this trade does not go as planned. After our trader has opened the position, GBP/USD drops and the stop loss order kicks in, resulting in the trade being exited for a loss of 75 points (1.6000 - 1.5925). Our trader has lost £150 on the trade so his trading pot now stands at £4850 (£5000 original size - £150 loss).

On his next trade, assuming he is going to stick to the 3% of pot risk rule, he will allow himself to risk losing £145.50. On his next trade, his analysis tells him to have a stop loss 100 points away from his entry point; he knows to stick to his position sizing rule so he should trade £1.45 per point (£145.50 risk / 100 points stop loss).

This can seem a very conservative approach to the new trader. And there is a reason for this: it is!

If your idea of trading is risking all on whether USD/JPY falls 50 points this morning then this approach is not for you (but if that is the case then chances are, once again, you won't be trading very long).

Until we actually start trading, I think it is safe to say that we all expect that our decisions are going to be not far off 100% right all the time. But the reality often falls short.

You do not need £5000 to start trading forex and you don't necessarily need to use 3% as your benchmark level of risk for your trades. But you should give some thought to the size of your positions and your ability to withstand a losing streak. In my experience most people don't – as I didn't in the beginning.

> ## Key point:
>
> Deciding how much to risk on any one trade is a critical part of the process. A little effort applied here, and subsequently adhered to, should help insulate you from one of the most common mistakes of trading too big and all the associated problems that brings.

Stop losses – managing the risk of being wrong

Once the position sizing is figured out, we can then think about starting to trade.

A big part of our trading strategy, as mentioned a few times already, will be having a plan to get out of the trade at a relatively small, manageable loss if things do not pan out as expected. This is where the stop loss order comes in.

Spread betting myths

There is a lot of rubbish talked about stop losses, so let's get some of the myths out of the way from the start.

First of all, some people are reluctant to place stop loss orders because the all-knowing market will somehow mystically know where their stop is, move to that point and stop them out for a loss, before proceeding in the direction the trader first thought the market was going to go. The variation on this is that the spread betting company, knowing where your stop loss is, will also move the market to that level, execute the stop and then the market will go back to where it was. If I had a crisp ten pound note for every time I had heard these excuses, I would be far too busy raking the sand on my Caribbean island to write a book about spread betting forex.

Markets do not magically move tens and hundreds of points against you to find your personal stop loss. Also, if a spread betting company moved a market 50 points to get your stop loss, do you not think there would be a host of clients only too willing to take this price because it is so out of whack with where the market is actually trading?

I am sure there is an internet conspiracy out there about how this would be possible, but let's just draw a line under the whole 'moving the market to take out the stops' fallacy, particularly when it comes to a market such as forex that sees so much volume on a daily basis. Yes, on the very odd occasion if you are a very, very sizeable trader in certain markets, and the market is very quiet, and if certain other sizeable traders have an inkling where you have placed your orders to exit a position, there is the possibility that they may try and push the market in that direction. But for those of us trading somewhere south of multi-million pound positions in the markets we do not need to concern ourselves.

Unfortunately this conspiracy rubbish is just one reason that people choose not to place stop losses.

The danger of too tight stops

Another reason is the excuse that stop losses have been used in the past, the trade got stopped out, and then the market went the way the trader was expecting all the time. I think with this excuse there is an element of selective memory playing its part. It will, of course, happen some of the time that we get stopped out at the absolute extreme of a move against us, only to see the market promptly reverse and go on to hit our target, but that is just a fact of trading life from time to time. But if you find yourself getting regularly stopped out, only to see the market promptly turn around and head off in the direction you were expecting it to in the first place, then it is usually not the stop loss that is at fault but the *placing* of the stop.

A common mistake for all of us at the beginning is to place stops far too tight.

Let's take a quiet day on GBP/USD as an example. On a day like this we may see the currency pair only move somewhere in the region of 50 points. This is a market just chopping around doing very little, with no real direction. Let's say our trader has decided to place a trade, expecting the market to rise 200 points over the next week and decides to place a stop 15 points way. Again, let's not exert our brain power thinking of the reason behind this, but just bear with me while we examine the mentality behind this thought process.

Our trader has decided to trade one of the biggest financial markets in the world. Fair enough. His analysis also tells him this market is going to go up. Again this is a fair enough opinion as no one has a crystal ball to know for sure which way GBP/USD is going to go. Trading is all about playing the probabilities. But – and this is the important bit – our trader is only giving the market the tiniest of chances, the slimmest margins of error, to prove him right.

A mere 15 points.

So the rationale our trader is putting in place for this trade is along the lines of:

"I think this market is going up and I expect it to start moving in my direction pretty much as soon as I place this trade."

What are the chances that he has pinpointed the exact moment when this market takes off? There is always the exception that will prove the rule but hopefully you would agree that on average it is going to be pretty slim.

Key point:

When placing stops, give some thought to the typical volatility for your chosen market – don't get taken out in the 'noise'.

The conclusion to draw here is that, regardless of what time frame you are trading, you need to give a market time to move around, and time to prove you right.

If, for example, you are looking to run a trade over a few days and you feel there is a potential profit of several hundred points, you want to avoid getting taken out in the hour-to-hour noise of the market.

All this is of course easier said than done, but giving some thought to placing stops can avoid you getting frustrated time and again by having them far too tight in relation to your entry point, when considering the normal volatility of that market.

Patience is another valuable quality when it comes to trading. Realising that just because *you* have decided a market is going to start a move of several hundred points, doesn't necessarily mean the market is going to fulfil your wishes immediately.

After risking too much on any one trade and then not placing stop losses, placing them too tight is probably the next biggest mistake we all make when starting to trade. So don't be afraid of having slightly wider stop losses if you are looking to catch a move over a few hours/days/weeks. Just remember to adjust your trade size (pound per point) to reflect this and keep the risk manageable.

[We will be coming back to the placing of stops when we look at some trading strategies.]

Key point:

Having a strategy for getting out of a trade if it doesn't go to plan is a critical part of your strategy. This should ideally be set when you place the trade and should be placed to give the market time to prove you're right, i.e. not too tight.

Types of stop order

Broadly speaking, when spread betting there are two types of stop available – the *normal* stop and the *guaranteed* stop. Usually, the normal stop has no charge to place, while the guaranteed stop attracts a charge in some way (typically by incurring a wider spread when you open and close the trade, a few more points either side of the usual bid/offer price).

Both types of stop have their merits. Depending on your attitude to risk you will probably prefer one over the other.

Let's look at the difference between them.

In all financial markets there is the risk of what is known as *slippage*. This is where your order ends up getting filled at a worse price than you were expecting – sometimes much worse if the market experiences a large 'gap'.

Example – stop loss order filled as expected

To show how stop loss orders will *usually* work, I have picked a random day's trading in GBP/USD. The chart below shows a fairly sideways day overall with a range of 100 points or so. Whenever GBP/USD slips back towards 1.5925 sentiment changes and we see the currency pair rally slightly.

Figure 3.1: GBP/USD 2 October 2009

So our trader may decide that GBP/USD is a buy down at current levels and decides to put the trade on. The low all day has been 1.5925 so a stop loss is placed below here, for example at 1.5915. Let's fast-forward a few hours and see what happened next.

Figure 3.2: GBP/USD 2 October 2009

Just before midnight, GBP/USD broke below that short-term support and traded as low as 1.5912. The stop loss would have kicked in and I would expect that trade to be closed out at the stop loss level of 1.5915. Over the course of the next hour or so the currency pair moved lower so our trader would have been glad he placed the stop – the trade was closed for a small, manageable loss.

Now, in my experience the vast majority of cases where stop losses get hit, the process above is what you can expect. The trade gets exited at the level you were expecting, you realise the planned loss and there is no drama.

However, there is always the problem of 'slippage' in financial markets. There is no rule that says a market has to trade in an orderly fashion – the price does not necessarily have to move in one point increments up or down. A market can experience jumps from one price to the next and these can be large or small. There are several factors that can make this happen.

For example: an economic report where the result ends up being very different to what the market was expecting (e.g. monthly unemployment numbers much worse/better than expected); an event that takes markets completely by surprise (e.g. government coup); or just a simple lack of liquidity available in a market (e.g. a larger than normal order hits a market). All of these events and more can cause markets to gap and this could mean your stop loss could end up getting filled at a worse price than expected.

Since forex is a 24-hour market with usually constant trading, the risk of slippage is less than in, say, stock markets. Of course, forex still shuts up for business on a Friday night and does not start again until Sunday evening, so there is a period when outside events cannot be factored in by the market as it happens and may produce a sharp reaction when the market re-opens.

You can occasionally get gaps during the day, as explained above, but in forex these sorts of gaps are rarer than in stock markets. However, there is a way, if you want to, of completely eliminating the risk of your stop loss order being filled at a worse than expected price – and this is the *guaranteed stop*.

Guaranteed stop loss

If you really want to absolutely control the possible loss on your trade right from the start you can use a guaranteed stop loss.

This gives you a level of risk control that is not easily available in the actual underlying market. With a guaranteed stop loss you are guaranteeing the level you will be stopped out at. Even if the currency pair you are trading gaps 100 points through your stop loss, you are still closed out at your specified level. This is why you will typically pay a slight premium (charged via a wider spread) when using them. This cost of the guarantee will vary from one market to another, and from one spread betting company to another, but some typical charges are shown in the following table.

Representative charges for guaranteed stop orders

Market	Typical spread	Extra spread for guaranteed stop
EUR/USD	2 points	3 points
GBP/USD	3 points	3 points
USD/JPY	3 points	3 points
EUR/GBP	3 points	3 points

Source: IG Index

In effect, you are buying insurance and like all forms of insurance it never comes free. But it does let you sleep easy, safe in the knowledge that if, for example, interest rates are doubled overnight, you are not going to end up with a bigger loss than you were expecting when you first placed the trade.

A relatively small price to pay

Many companies now offer accounts that force you to place a guaranteed stop loss when you actually place the trade. No bad idea for those who are new to spread betting and for the more volatile markets such as forex.

As mentioned previously this extra insurance is usually charged by adding a few points onto either side of the spread – and when we are talking about markets that can move in excess of a hundred points a day this is fairly inconsequential in the great scheme of things.

On the other hand of course, if you are going to be a very active trader these few extra points can all add up over time. It is all down to individual attitude to risk and risk management that will determine whether you want to use guaranteed stops or trade using normal stops and take the extra risk of slippage in your stride.

It would be fair to say that many experienced traders, particularly in very liquid markets such as forex, do not use guaranteed stop losses and stick to the normal stop loss. That is my own preferred way of handling the risk. It is down to your own personal attitude to risk control which one you use. My only advice, if you hadn't guessed already, would be that a stop loss in one shape or other *should* be used on all trades.

For those new to spread betting and trading forex I would strongly urge you to make sure your stop loss is in place with your spread betting company when the trade is live. If you get into the discipline of doing this it means you free up your time from watching the screen constantly, and also hopefully reduces the risk of you changing your mind on closing out the trade when it goes against you.

We will come back to stop losses at some length again in the chapter on trading strategies.

Risk versus reward – is the trade really worth doing?

When it comes to trading, there are many ways to lose money!

First of all, you could risk everything on one trade. Trade far too big for the size of your account and stubbornly stick your head in the sand as the market moves against you, until you are forced to close out your trade – or have it closed for you – having lost all your trading pot. (This is far more common than you might think.)

On the other hand, you could trade relatively small on each trade and have a never-ending losing run. Never-ending, that is, until your account is down to zero.

But probably the most common way – and a mistake that lots of us make, at least in the beginning – is to have a reasonable balance of winners to losers, but still end up losing money. We may even, to add insult to injury, have been right more times than we have been wrong.

How can this be?

It is all down to the risk versus reward of our trades.

Getting the balance wrong

Where most of us go wrong when we start off is having quite a few small profits, but then having some chunky losing trades that take away those profits – and a bit more. So after a lot of effort and a few trades, we are in the red. It is the old cliché about trading:

> *let your profits run, cut your losses quickly*

completely turned on its head.

The trader is nervous that his open profits are going to be taken away, so snatches at them as soon as the market shows the faintest sign of starting to move against the position and take away the hard-earned profit. And then, on the flip side, the eternally optimistic view on a losing trade: that the market will come back. But of course sometimes it doesn't, and a manageable loss gets bigger and bigger as the trader continues to practise denial and hope the position will recover. It is a very dangerous spiral to get caught in and has more to do with gambling than calm, calculated risk-taking.

Let's take another one of those steps back and think about what a profitable trading strategy looks like.

You don't have to be right all the time

As I have mentioned before, I think we all start off with an over-inflated view of our ability to predict which way the market is going; and unless we lose the 'I-am-always-right' attitude we could well be setting ourselves up for a spectacular failure further down the road. Being profitable over the long run does not necessarily equate to having to be right all the time. If we have a strategy that is right just half the time, but when it is correct it makes £200, and when it is wrong it only loses £100 – then that is a profitable strategy.

So I would suggest we can all do ourselves a favour by giving some thought to the potential risk versus reward make-up of trades, before our itchy fingers get to click buy or sell. A couple of minutes running through our objectives for the trade can save a lot of grief further down the line and help to eliminate some of the dodgy trades – meaning we end up only concentrating on the stronger opportunities.

Weighing up the risk-reward ratio involves figuring out whether the trade is worth taking: is the potential profit really worth the potential loss we are willing to incur?

Example – would you take this trade?

Let's look at an example of a potential trade (we will stick with GBP/USD for now). The following chart represents two days of trading for the currency pair.

Figure 3.3: GBP/USD – risk reward

Without worrying at the moment about any particular analysis technique, we will assume that our trader has decided GBP/USD is going up and it is currently 1.6458 to buy.

Sensibly, a stop loss is going to be set and the trader decides this is to be set at below the current day's low. The low was around 1.6380 – so the stop is set a little below here, choosing to place it at 1.6370. When it comes to thinking about a profit target, again our trader is going to be conservative and decides that profits will be taken if GBP/USD gets back to the previous day's high, which is at 1.6560.

Let's work out the risk-reward ratio on this trade. An easy enough calculation to make but one that many people will not even bother considering.

The risk is simply the entry point minus the stop loss level – assuming, of course, that no slippage is experienced on the trade. So the calculation is 1.6458 - 1.6370. If the trade ends up being wrong, the loss will be 88 points.

When it comes to the potential reward, again this is a simple calculation. The trader has decided that the trade will be exited at the previous day's high, so the maximum profit potential is that level minus the entry point: 1.6560 – 1.6458, which translates into 102 points.

Trade summary – risk reward example

Variable	Value
Trade entry price	1.6458
Stop loss	1.6370
Potential loss	88 (1.6458 - 1.6370)
Target price for exit	1.6560
Potential profit	102 (1.6560 - 1.6458)
Reward/risk ratio	1.2

Now we have broken the trade down into how much potential profit we are going to get for the risk, does it appeal to you?

The trader is looking at risking losing 88 points to make 102 points. To me, it definitely does not look to be an opportunity that makes that much financial sense. But people will make trades like this, and worse, every day.

As I have mentioned numerous times already, many people ignore this aspect of trading because of an overconfidence in their own abilities to predict where they think the market is going to go. In practice, no one can predict the future with 100% accuracy. Trading is all about trying to stack the odds in our favour, and many people think that an important part of that process boils down to getting the risk versus reward right on the trade.

Is there an ideal risk versus reward ratio?

Ideally, you want the potential profit from your trade to be some multiple of your potential risk. This means doing a realistic evaluation of the profit potential – without tweaking the numbers to make this fit!

Whether you go for two, three, four or some other multiple of the risk as potential reward, is down to you. A popular suggestion is to look for at least three times the risk as potential reward on the trade and this is still a yardstick that I personally stick by.

Spending a little time on weighing up the true risk-reward ratio of the trade (and as mentioned above, not massaging the figures to make it look better than it really is) is time well spent. It can help weed out the 'fifty-fifty, flip-a-coin' type trades, where you are risking too much to make too little. It can also help you refine the entry point of trades. If you are a little more patient, is there a chance the trade can get executed at a better level and improve the risk versus reward? This is where orders can come in: where you place an order to buy or sell at a certain level, freeing you up from watching the screen all the time.

We will come back to the idea of identifying good risk versus reward trades, and also using orders, when we get into trading strategies in the next section. Like position sizing, risk versus reward is one of those factors that should be given thought before trading. It should become second nature on every trade done.

Key point:

Weighing up whether a trade is really worth taking should be an important part of your decision-making process. It doesn't have to take too long, but a little effort spent before opening a trade can ensure that you really are focussing on strong opportunities rather than just, effectively, flipping a coin.

Technical Analysis

My background is in technical analysis (sometimes called charting), best described as the study of previous price action in a financial market to *try* and forecast the future direction of that market. The UK has an official body in this area, the Society of Technical Analysts (STA). Every year the STA holds exams and passing these is a recognised qualification in financial markets. I sat and passed the STA exams in 1995.

So I am a big fan of looking at charts when it comes to deciding on whether there is a trading opportunity in a market. However, I also appreciate there is no such thing as a Holy Grail trading system that is right all the time. New traders can do themselves a big favour, and save an awful lot of time at the beginning, if they accept this.

Technical analysis is very popular with traders all around the world, and probably no more so than in the forex market. All technical analysis techniques are, to one extent or another, the study of mass market psychology, and what better place to apply this than the biggest financial market in the world.

Before looking at some strategies, let's go through some of the basics of charting.

Different ways of displaying price data

Probably the simplest chart is a line chart which just shows one type of data (typically the closing price for that particular period) at regular intervals.

Line charts

The following chart is a line chart over a one year period for USD/JPY. It is a *daily* chart – this means that only the closing price in this example is shown for every day. Of course, with forex we do not have an official close to the market (as it trades 24 hours) so the closing price shown on the spread betting companies' daily charts will typically be the price at midnight, UK time.

This series of closing prices is plotted on the chart and a line is drawn to connect the points. Even though this is the most basic way of showing price data, it is still a useful method of displaying historic prices. For example, it is easy to spot the trends over various periods.

Figure 4.1: simple line chart, daily close

Sticking with line charts, we do not of course have to limit these to just the longer-term perspective, it is perfectly possible to display short-term price data using a line chart. The example below is a two day line chart with *10 minute* intervals. This means that the closing price is taken at the end of each ten minute period throughout the day. Once again these points are joined up with a line making it clear where the market traded over the two day period shown.

Figure 4.2: line chart, 10-minute interval

Line charts are a perfectly adequate way of looking at price data. When it comes to looking at markets from a longer-term perspective, some people prefer them because they filter out a lot of the short-term noise for the market in question.

But, for most people looking at charts, the line chart tends to be passed over in favour of a couple of other ways of showing the data. Which brings us to bars and candlesticks.

Bar charts

For many years, the chart of choice for chartists was the bar chart. This is what a bar looks like:

Figure 4.3: bar chart

Whereas a line chart only shows one point of price data for the time period in question (typically the closing price, as mentioned) bar charts show the close plus also the high, the low and the open. The small horizontal mark to the left on the bar is the opening price, the mark to the right is the closing price, and the extremes of the vertical bar represent the high and the low traded for that particular time frame.

For example, with reference to the preceding chart, on 28 July (represented by the third bar in the chart), GBP/USD opened at 16,485, closed at 16,404 and during the day reached a high of 16,556 and a low of 16,390.

If a chart is a daily chart then the bar shows the open, high, low, close (OHLC) for the day, and if it is a ten minute interval chart then a new bar is drawn every ten minutes showing the OHLC for that period.

Bars grew in popularity as traders became more short-term focussed. If trades were going to be placed using relatively tight stop losses then it became more important to know the absolute high or low traded in a particular period. Whereas, if the price is represented as a line chart there is only one price used. The price may have ended today roughly where it finished the previous day, which would result in little change on the line chart, but if it had swung around in a 200 point range all day that would not be seen on the chart. Bar charts let traders see the range traded for the time period in question.

Candlestick charts

Over the last 15 years or so many chartists have turned to a slightly different way of displaying the price data – which brings us to the candlestick chart. Candlestick charting is thought to date back to the 1600s and, if so, can be considered as the earliest form of technical analysis. It has enjoyed a resurgence since the mid-1990s – all the charts I look at are candles.

Candlesticks still use the raw OHLC data to display what the market in question has been doing. But with candlestick charting, the difference between the open and close is considered important and this gets 'blocked in' when the candlestick is constructed.

Here is a bar and a candle showing exactly the same market, GBP/USD, over the same time period.

Figure 4.4: bar chart

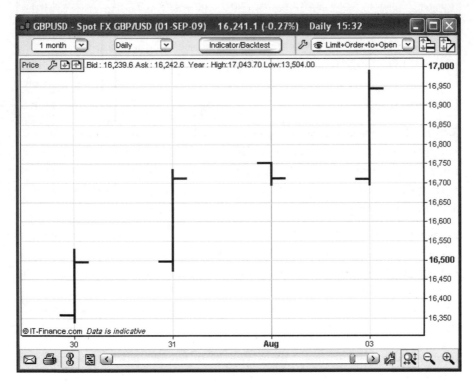

Figure 4.5: candlestick chart (for the same data as the previous chart)

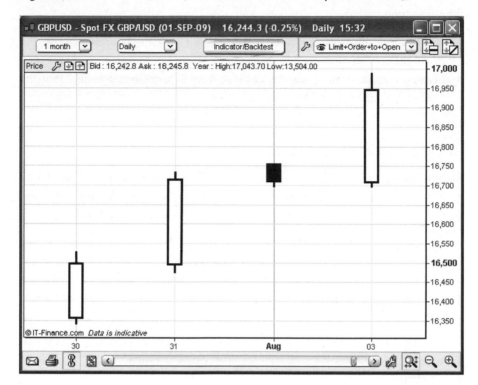

The blocked in part of the candle shows the difference between the open and the close on the day, and is referred to as the *body* of the candlestick. The extremes, which look like wicks on a candle, are referred to as *shadows*. Look at the last candlestick on the chart (on the right-hand side). As this is an *up day* (i.e. the market closed higher than it opened) the candlestick traditionally gets coloured in white; on a *down day* (the second candle from the right) the tradition is for a black body.

> Most charting packages now let you pick whatever colours you want, with red and green being popular default choices.

Keep it simple

A common approach to learning about technical analysis is to start with the basics (support, resistance, trends, patterns, etc.) and to then move onto the more mathematical approaches (such as the various moving averages and oscillators). Human nature being what it is there is a tendency to feel that the more complicated approaches must be better.

Why?

Well, because they are a bit more complicated of course...

Unfortunately, as a result many of the basic principles can end up being ignored in the search for the perfect indicators to build the foolproof trading system that will churn out money by the bucket-load on a regular basis.

In my opinion it is a shame that many of us take this approach in the beginning. It can be an expensive approach too. I think the siren song of the perfect indicator is a tempting one for all of us, but I firmly believe that the basic principles of technical analysis can form the cornerstone of many trading strategies.

So I make no apologies by starting off the next part (on strategies) with that most basic form of market analysis: support and resistance.

Part Two

Trading Strategies

Now we get to the meaty bit of the book:

1. analysing the markets,

2. planning our trade,

3. calculating the risk-reward ratio and size of the position,

4. executing the trade and monitoring it, and

5. managing the position.

As I have mentioned in the previous chapters, there's a fair bit more to trading than just clicking buy or sell. By the time we get to the stage of placing the first trade we should already have decided on:

1. how big our trading pot is,

2. how much we are willing to risk on each trade,

3. what sort of time frame we intend trading, and

4. what level of risk-reward ratio we are looking for.

If those decisions have not been made, then we are setting ourselves up for failure at the first hurdle.

But assuming that you have been diligent (and not just skipped ahead to this chapter looking for the Holy Grail), let's think about our trading strategies.

Support and Resistance

What better place to start off looking at where a market may go than by examining where it has been? For many this is the purest form of market analysis: looking at the raw price data and just focussing on what the market in question has been doing over the time frame they are interested in.

The first part of this basic chart analysis is the idea of support and resistance. As anyone even mildly interested in the markets will know, prices seldom move in a straight, vertical line up and down. Even if a market is experiencing a definite trend in one direction, there will be a series of moves both in the direction of the trend and against it that make up this overall rise and fall. This creates the idea of different levels on the chart – typically showing troughs and peaks – which are referred to as support and resistance.

These levels show areas where sentiment swung from positive to negative, or vice versa, and where the market changed direction.

There is no mysticism behind how support and resistance gets formed. If GBP/USD has been rising and, for example, gets as high as 1.7000 (see the following chart), and then turns and drops back to 1.6400, it's showing where positive sentiment evaporated and the consensus view of market participants changed. Put in plain English: it stopped going up and started going down.

Figure 5.1: GBP/USD – support and resistance

So the market has drawn a clear line in the sand at 1.7000. At this level GBP/USD was considered overpriced because the selling has become more aggressive than the buying and the price has dropped. As a result, the 1.7000 level is subsequently called a *resistance level*.

Let's say when it gets back down to 1.6400 the market rallies and a base is formed – this is known as *support*. If over the next few weeks the price climbs by a few hundred points, again the market is showing us clearly where sentiment has shifted, and those with a bullish view (positive) have gained the upper hand.

You see this play out time and again, across all markets and all different time frames. It is just raw market psychology. The actions of buyers and sellers causing the financial market in question to move up and down.

This is all well and good, and very easy to spot in hindsight. Unfortunately, however, I have yet to find a spread betting company that lets its clients go back and trade off prices in the past. (If you are fortunate enough to know of someone who allows these *Tardis trades* be sure to let me know...)

But support and resistance can give us clues for potential levels to watch in the future – and indicate a trading *set-up*.

By **set–up** I mean something that is happening on the chart that flags the potential for a trade. It is when the market starts doing something that we have previously defined is part of our trading strategy – so it can be a combination of factors that highlights to us it is time to think about opening up a new trade.

The basic principle

One of the principles behind support and resistance is that levels that were important in the past could well be important again in the future.

This seems a reasonable assumption. The idea of support and resistance is all about identifying areas where the concept of price was accepted or rejected.

If something rises to 500 then drops – the view was it was overpriced. If it drops to 400 then goes back to 500, then at 400 the consensus opinion was that it was under-priced. This sort of action, caused by the behaviour of buyers and sellers, plays out all day long in the markets.

Putting the principle into action

One very simplistic approach – but no less worthwhile for being simple – is to look to buy when a price approaches previous support, and sell when it fails ahead of previous resistance.

Like all strategies this is not going to work all the time, but it can help set up good risk versus reward trading opportunities.

First of all, of course, we need to be able to quantify our risk and decide where the stop loss is going to go. An advantage of trading using support and resistance levels is that they can help when it comes to deciding on setting the stop loss.

If we have decided that a certain level is a barrier to the market (whether on the way up or the way down) and we are going to place a trade to take advantage of this, when does the reason for the trade become invalid?

When that barrier is broken.

Let's think about this. A level of support that has been propping the market up is recognised as support because every time the market weakens back to here the consensus view is that it is under-priced. If, however, it breaks through the level then the market clearly does not think it is under-priced anymore because it is still falling. So our reason for buying is no longer there. This is why it is the *break* of support or resistance that suggests the trade should be closed for a small loss – and why the stop loss goes below support and correspondingly of course, above resistance when selling short.

I make no apologies for the simplicity of this approach.

Of course there are more involved analyses of markets that can be done, and we will come to some of those a bit later. But as support and resistance is the most basic part of price information we get from a market, it seems foolish to ignore it.

Now let's look at some real world examples.

Support and resistance – Example 1

As this is the first example, we are going to take it slowly and go step-by-step through every process of the trade:

1. initial market analysis

2. trade planning

3. executing the trade

4. monitoring and managing the trade

5. the exit

This first example is GBP/USD in the first few months of 2009. We are using a candlestick chart where each candle represents one day of trading.

Figure 5.2: example trade 1 – support and resistance

1. Initial market analysis

We can see that it has been a volatile few months for the GBP/USD currency pair. At the beginning of the period we're looking at it has traded as high as 1.5400, before dropping down to the 1.3500 mark by the fourth week of January. This is a 1900 point move (1.5400 - 1.3500). The driver behind this was the ongoing credit crunch and the UK government's continued bailout of the banking sector – the net result was that the pound slipped to its lowest level in more than 20 years against the US dollar.

But from this low, into February, there was a clear change in sentiment. The balance of power shifted from the sellers to the buyers and GBP/USD rose – the pound recovered against the US dollar. It rallied as high as 1.4985 by 9 February, a rise of almost 1500 points from the 1.3500 low.

The balance of power then shifted once again and by the second week of March, GBP/USD was back below 1.4000.

Some obvious support and resistance levels

Going back to the basic principles that we have been looking at: the market has left us with some very clear, slap-you-in-the-face levels. To my eyes there is some obvious support and resistance on this chart where market sentiment has clearly swung from one extreme to another.

When the market got near 1.3500 in late January the view was clearly (in hindsight) that the slide was overdone and there was value down here. So the price rose. This pushed GBP/USD up nearly 1500 points to trade at 1.4985. Then once again up here market perception changed and GBP/USD was viewed as too expensive.

How do we know this?

Well it stopped going up and started going down!

Figure 5.3: example trade 1 – support and resistance

We have two clear lines in the sand on this chart, and if we are using the concept of support and resistance to identify our trades then we just may have a trading set-up based on where the price is at the moment.

We know that when the market was down below 1.4000 last time, it did not stay down here for too long and the price bounced back. Going on the principle of support and resistance (where levels that were important in the past are expected to be important in the future) we may favour the probability of another bounce from this area.

Looking for additional confirmation

But blindly buying as a price approaches potential support (or selling when it heads towards potential resistance) can be a dangerous strategy if that particular trend is strong. The textbook approach would be to wait for at least some sign of a turnaround ahead of what we perceive as being an important level for the market.

In this example I think we have it.

The final candle on the chart shows that during this day (today, for the purposes of our hypothetical trade) the market did push lower but has ended the day as a white candle. This shows the close on the day was higher than the open, so we have seen a shift in sentiment during the day – the market has not carried on blindly lower.

Right. So that's it, isn't it?

Let's pile in, £500 per point and wait for the cash to start rolling in...

2. Trade planning

Of course, if you are sensible, that is not just it. We need to take some time to think through this trade and see if it is worth doing – and then work out how big the trade should be.

First of all, the risk side of the equation. Back in January, GBP/USD traded down to 1.3500 before rallying, so this is the support level.

Where should our stop loss go?

Well, if we think that 1.3500 is an important level and the reason behind this trade, then by definition there is no point us still being in the trade if 1.3500 is broken. I am going to choose a stop loss 30 points below here (an arbitrary amount) for this. So our stop is going in at 1.3470.

Now, the reward consideration: just how much potential profit do we think, going by the chart, there could be if this trade pans out as expected? Rather than dreaming up an imaginary figure to make this look like the most attractive trade in the world, the best indication we have is what happened last time around. And back then, the market rallied to 1.4985. So I would suggest our target goes up around there. I am going to err on the side of being conservative and set 1.4900 as the objective for this trade.

Risk-reward calculation

So we have our trade set-up; we know our stop; we know our target. It is time to calculate if, at the current level where the market is trading, the trade looks good from a risk-reward point of view:

- At the moment the market is 1.3850 to buy. If our stop loss is going in at 1.3470 then the **risk** is 380 points (1.3850 - 1.3470) – if we are wrong, that will be our loss.

- And again if we are buying at 1.3850 with an objective of 1.4900 for the trade, then the potential **reward** is 1050 points (1.4900 - 1.3850).

What's the risk versus reward?

It is, of course, an easy calculation. If we are willing to risk losing 380 points to make 1050 points then the calculation is 1050/380 which comes out as 2.76. Our potential profit on this trade is 2.76 times bigger than the potential risk.

Trade plan summary

Variable	Value
Trade direction	Long
Entry price	1.3850
Stop level	1.3470
Potential loss	380 (1.3850 - 1.3470)
Target level for exit	1.4900
Potential profit	1050 (1.4900 - 1.3850)
Reward-risk ratio	2.76 (1050/380)

Would you be happy with this potential?

It is by no means a bad R:R. It is down to individual preferences, but many approaches recommend aiming for a risk reward of at least 3. That would personally be what I would be looking for out of the trade. Which leaves us with a dilemma on this one:

Where do we get in?

Calculation for a target risk-reward ratio

There's a very easy calculation you can do if you have the stop and target of your trade, but are looking for an entry point that gives you a certain risk reward. Here is how it works.

I want to find out the 3:1 risk reward entry point for this trade. My target is 1.4900 and my stop is 1.3470. To find out my 3:1 point all I need to find out is the difference between the stop and the target, divide by 4 and then add this amount to the stop.

The target of 1.4900 minus the stop of 1.3470 gives us a value of 1430 points. Divided by four this equals 357.5 points. If I add this to my stop level of 1.3470 then the value is 1.3827 (we will ignore the extra .5 on the end).

So now we have the ideal entry point if we want a potential reward of three times the risk on this trade. If we buy at 1.3827 then the risk is 357 points (1.3827 - 1.3470) and the potential reward is 1073 (1.4900 - 1.3827).

But of course the market is not trading at the preferred entry point, it is at 1.3850, so 23 points higher. Let's worry about that in a second. Next we have to decide how big we are going to trade – the all-important position sizing calculation.

Position sizing calculation

We have decided to execute this trade at 1.3827 to give us a risk reward of 3:1 based on our stop loss and target for the trade. The level for the stop loss is 1.3470, giving a risk of 357 points. We will assume that we have already decided that, on any one trade, if it goes wrong it is only going to lose £200. So to figure out how big we are going to trade this one we divide the amount of money we are willing to risk by the number of points potential loss: £200/357, which gives a figure of 0.56.

So on this trade, with a 357 point stop loss, if we are going to keep our loss to a manageable £200 based on the size of our account, we need to buy 56p per point.

3. Executing the trade

We are almost there.

We know our stop, our target, the size of our trade and our entry point.

The one problem is, of course, that the market is not currently at that entry point... it is trading slightly above it.

We have a couple of choices. One of these is to watch the screen, with our finger hovering over the buy button and wait for GBP/USD to hit 1.3827. But forex is a 24-hour market and it may take a while (if it happens at all) for the market to come back to our preferred level. If this is our approach we may need to stock up on the caffeine and move our PC into the bathroom ready for our around-the-clock vigil.

An altogether more sensible approach is to place an order with our spread betting company to do the trade at the required level. We can place an order to buy, 56p per point, at 1.3827.

> Technically this is referred to as a **limit order** – meaning you want to buy GBP/USD *at this price or better.* Some companies ask you to specify this as a limit order, with others you will not need to – you will just need to enter the amount you want to buy and at what price, and their systems will figure it out as a limit order because of where the market is currently trading in relation to your order price.

Most spread betting companies will also let you attach the stop loss order at this point as well (i.e. while you are setting up the order to buy in) – and this should be done if available. Once this is all done we have an order to buy at our preferred level, so we can head off and do something far more productive, instead of sitting and watching all the pretty colours flash on the trading screen.

What happened next?

The next day GBP/USD sold off initially, hitting 1.3700 at its lowest point before rallying to finish that day at 1.3920 (see following chart).

Figure 5.4: example trade 1 – support and resistance

Our order would have been filled on the way down. Our stop loss was not threatened. The market rebounded and we ended the day still in the trade and almost 100 points in profit.

Let's take a breather here before we see how the trade developed further.

You can see that there are a few other things to consider other than just how pretty the chart looks and it is time for a trade. And even to me, having written all of the previous paragraphs about planning the trade, working out the stop, the target, the risk reward and the position size, it feels like an awful lot of work! But it really isn't. Once you have identified the potential of a trading opportunity, all of the planning we have just been though will really only take a short time.

But it is important to spend the time figuring out whether the trade is worth doing and it can act as a sanity check on just jumping in and trading blindly.

One final word about the stop loss for this trade.

Some people may have read through the strategy and be sitting there thinking:

That is a chunky old distance to have a stop loss.

Yes, 300-odd points is a big number. But don't forget in this example we are looking for a fairly significant move, so it is not too over-ambitious based on the chart. If we are going for big moves then we need to give the market room to chop around.

If you look back at the chart, that big black down candle a couple of days before our trade set-up was signalled gave the range of GBP/USD on just one day in excess of 400 points. If we are going to trade volatile markets, we need to give them room to breathe when the trade is on.

Later, we will take a look at some more short-term examples that use tighter stops. But don't forget that setting really tight stops can be a false economy in markets that move. It is all about balance.

4. Monitoring and managing the trade

Let's get back to the trade.

We are one day in and the order has been filled. Our stop is in place and the trade at the moment is around 100 points in profit.

That sounds like a lot of profit. Shall we take it...?

No!

When we put this trade on, we were looking for 1073 points of profit from the entry point. The 100 points profit achieved so far is a mere drop in the ocean. Earlier in the book I highlighted that a common mistake is to be unable to resist taking quick profits – which end up being smaller than the losses. Patience is a virtue when it comes to trying to catch the bigger moves.

The difficult part of trading is this bit now: managing the trade.

The difficult bit

The process of buying or selling is easy. It is the bit in the middle that is tricky. If we get into a trade and it moves against us instantly and our stop gets triggered, then there is no thinking to do. The trade is closed for a small manageable loss and we move on.

But when the trade is moving in the right direction we need to start thinking about how much leeway to give the market. How much of our existing profit (so far unrealised), we are willing to give back to make more profit.

As with many things in trading, there is no absolute black or white way of doing this. We will rarely get out at the absolute extreme point of a move in our favour. It will be either exited too early when there was still money to be made, or too late when too much existing profit was given back. Bearing this in mind, there is an approach that I have used over the years that has worked for me which we will use for this example trade.

Moving the stop

When a trade starts to go into profit it can be tempting to move the stop loss very quickly to the break even point (i.e. to the point where the trade was opened). This is a perfectly valid technique for many people and if it works for you as part of an overall strategy and makes you money then that is the name of the game.

But the frustrating part of this approach is you can end up getting stopped out with zero or a small profit, and then the market carries on the way you thought it was going to go, but without you onboard. This approach can help our egos because we can avoid taking a loss – but it does mean we then need to think about getting back in again at another point.

[Did I mention before there is no Holy Grail...?]

How close should the stop be moved?

I still think the stop needs to be moved to lock in profits as the trade progresses, but personally I favour giving the market a bit more leeway to prove me right. So, not rushing to move it to the entry point too quickly.

Here's what I do.

If, when you put the trade on, your stop loss was, for example, 100 points away from your entry point, then the market should move at least 100 points in your favour before you consider moving the stop loss to the break even point.

Let's apply this approach to the current trade.

To recap, we are in at 1.3827 with a stop loss at 1.3470, which is 357 points away. Our target is 1.4900. If we are not going to move the stop loss to break even until (and, of course, if) the market has moved at least 357 points in our favour, then we need do nothing until the market is at 1.4184 (1.3827 + 357).

Let's see what the market did next.

Figure 5.5: example trade 1 – support and resistance

Over the course of the next three days the trade continues to move in our favour. We check the market once a day: in the evenings after work, for example. We have the stop in place to manage the risk. We are looking for a move that is probably going to take days and even weeks to come right, and watching it every second of the day is not going to make it go up any quicker – trust me!

We can see the market has moved more than 357 points in our favour, so decide to move the stop to the break even point.

This can be done by logging onto your spread betting platform and changing the level of the stop loss or, if you are feeling particularly lazy, calling up the spread betting company and asking for it to be moved. There should be no charge for moving the stop loss.

So the stop loss is now at break even – at the entry point of the trade, 1.3827. In effect, we now have a free trade: if it goes against us from here we will be out at no loss, barring any slippage on the stop.

We are now back to the mundane task of monitoring the trade.

Figure 5.6: example trade 1 – support and resistance

The next day is a quiet one but after that you can see a big move the following day: the market traded in a range of almost 500 points. The low for the day was 1.3843. So at one point during the day our profit on the trade was virtually reduced to zero. We gave back almost all the open profit on the trade, only to see the market bounce back and finish up at 1.4282. Our open profit at the end of this day was 455 points.

You can see how managing the trade is the difficult bit.

If we had our stop loss any tighter on this trade we would have been taken out (admittedly for a profit), only to see the market much higher at the end of the day. As it turns out, our stop was not taken out and we are still in the position with a fair old profit for our efforts so far.

Because the market has clearly pushed higher once again, I think it is time to think about locking in some profit.

Locking in some profit

As ever, there is always a dilemma faced when moving the stop loss during a trade to lock in some profit. On the one hand there is giving the market enough room to move around in its daily fluctuations so you do not get taken out in the noise of the market and remain in the trade to take advantage of further profits. And the flip side of this is not setting your stop loss so far away that a significant portion of the existing profit is lost.

It won't be surprising to learn that there is no easy answer to this, but here's one approach.

When the trade was first entered into, the potential reward was three times the maximum risk. Now the trade is running and in profit it still makes sense to have a sensible risk reward balance, but maybe give the market a bit more room to move around. So far, GBP/USD has been as high as 1.4282. This still leaves another 618 points to the target of 1.4900.

So the question is: how much profit should we risk sacrificing to squeeze out that extra 618 points?

One approach would be to look at it again from a risk reward point of view. Some would suggest risking giving back half of the additional potential profit and use this as a point to raise the stop loss to.

Let's walk through that approach for this trade.

The highest point reached has been 1.4282, leaving another 618 points to our target. Half of the extra potential profit that we feel is left in this trade would be 309 points. So, the stop loss would be placed at 1.4282 - 309 points, which means the stop gets moved to 1.3973. We are willing to sacrifice 309 points of unrealised profit to try and make an additional 618 points, giving a risk reward balance of two to one.

Stop calculation

Variable	Value
Trade direction	Long
Target price for exit	1.4900
Highest price reached so far	1.4282
Distance left to target price	618 (1.4900 - 1.4282)
Distance left to target price / 2	309
New stop level	1.3973 (1.4282 - 309)

I would not claim this is an ideal solution, mainly because I don't think there is one, but it can serve as a method of gradually ratcheting up your stop order to come out of the trade, as the market approaches the target.

Let's assume that we have moved the stop to 1.3973 and see what happens next.

Figure 5.7: example trade 1 – support and resistance

Once again the market has moved in the right direction for the trade. So, once again, we should think about moving the stop to lock in profit.

On this last day the market got as high as 1.4595, so it is now 305 points away from our target. Assuming we are willing to risk half of this amount to stay in the trade and try to achieve our ultimate target, then our stop gets moved to 1.4595 - 158 (which is half of the distance left to the target). This means our stop order is moved to 1.4437.

You can see that as the market gets closer and closer to our target, the stop is getting moved tighter towards the highest point reached in the trade so far. Ultimately, the risk of tightening the stop so much means that we could just get taken out in the day-to-day noise of the market.

Let's see what the next day brought.

Figure 5.8: example trade 1 – support and resistance

The black candle at the extreme right of the chart represents the following day – you can see what a relatively quiet day it was by the size of the candle. But during the day, the market traded down to 1.4395, which would have taken us out of the trade as our stop was placed at 1.4437.

The trade is closed for a profit, so let's see how we did.

5. The exit

We bought 56p per point at 1.3827 and got 'profit-stopped' at 1.4437. So the points profit on this trade was 610. This equates to a cash profit of £341.60 (56p per point x 610 points) before financing costs. Although not exact, I estimate that for this trade, running over eight days, the financing would have been no more than £7. Overall we would have ending up making around £334 from this trade.

Trade profit/loss summary

Variable	Value
Entry price	1.3827
Trade size (£ per point)	0.56
Exit price	1.4437
Points made	610 (1.4437 - 1.3827)
Profit (£)	341.60 (£0.56 x 610)

The actual risk reward achieved ended up being less than our targeted amount of 3 to 1. The risk was £200 and our profit was £334, so we ended up making 1.67 times our potential loss.

While this isn't the best outcome, is there anything we could have done to make it better?

As the trade progressed we could have moved the stop loss tighter to avoid giving back too much of our open profit. But with the market as volatile as it was, if we had started doing this as soon as our trade was in profit, we would have been stopped out at break even or, at best, with a fraction of the profit achieved.

One approach, if you are convinced of the validity of your target, is to leave the stop loss in the original position when you started the trade and only exit when and if the market actually touches your target. From a purist point of view this makes sense – if you are that convinced of your target you should hang in there. But from a practical point of view it means that if there is, for example, just 50 points left to your target, you are risking giving back hundreds of points just to achieve that extra sliver of profit.

Like I said, there is no perfect tactic for this and any trade management technique is going to have an element of compromise.

Personally, I like the one outlined here as a reasonable compromise between sacrificing some profit and trying to hit the original target. It is one of those things that you can really start to develop when you start trading – you will get a feeling for which approach is the right one for you.

To wrap up this first trade example, let's see what happened with GBP/USD subsequently...

Figure 5.9: example trade 1 – support and resistance

During the days after our trade was stopped for a profit, the market did push higher (as far as 1.4775) so only 125 points away from the ultimate target. But then it reversed sharply back towards 1.4100 before eventually getting back to 1.4900 by the first week of April.

Overall, the trade worked out well in this example. Although writing it all down step-by-step has proved to be quite long-winded, I hope you have found it useful. It highlights the key points that need to be considered both before and during a trade – and once you start trading for real, they should become second nature and be only a matter of a few minutes work.

Now we have that epic out of the way, let's take a look at a couple of other set-ups in different time frames, but still using the principle of support and resistance.

Support and resistance – Example 2

For this example, we will look at a different currency pair and a shorter term time frame – to illustrate that the idea of support and resistance levels happens across all markets and all periods.

The chart shown is another candlestick chart, this time of the Australian dollar/US dollar pair (AUD/USD). It is a two hour chart, meaning that each candlestick shows a two-hour period of trading (when the two hours are up, a new candlestick is drawn). The chart shows the first couple of weeks trading for AUD/USD in August 2009.

Figure 5.10: example trade 2 – support and resistance

Market analysis

Looking at this chart, it is clear where sentiment has changed over the past couple of weeks for this particular currency pair. In early August we can see some sideways trading going on, with AUD/USD getting as high as the 0.8470 mark on 4 August and then subsequent pushes back, running out of steam. Eventually a bigger sell-off is seen and the Aussie drops back to 0.8180 by 12 August.

Sentiment switches again and AUD/USD rallies quite sharply back towards the previous highs. The last candlestick on the chart shows possibly the first signs of nervousness sneaking back in ahead of the 0.8470 level. The market pushes back to here but then quickly retreats.

Here's the trade we're going to look at.

Trade planning

This time a *short* trade, looking for weakness back to the lows of 12 August. Sticking to the basic principles of support and resistance: if levels that were important in the past are going to be important in the future then AUD/USD should not break the 0.8470 level, so the stop needs to go above here. As usual we will allow for a small margin of error and set the stop at 0.8490.

The target for the trade would seem to be clear: a run back to the lows earlier in the month. So we will set the target at 0.8200. If we assume that our trader is looking for a risk reward entry point of at least 3:1, the calculation is a simple one.

The stop at 0.8490 and the target of 0.8200 gives us a distance of 290 points between these two levels. This value divided by four results in a value of 72.5. So the 3:1 entry point for this trade can be calculated by subtracting that from the stop. This means that 8490 - 72.5 gives us a value of 8417.5. So we will set the order to sell at 0.8418.

With a stop loss at 0.8490 and an entry point of 0.8418, our risk in terms of points is 72. Again, our trader only wants to risk losing £200 on this trade if it does not turn out as expected and the stop is hit. So the size for the trade per point is £200/72, which means that AUD/USD should be sold at £2.77 per point.

Trade parameter summary

Variable	Value
Trade direction	Short
Target price for exit	0.8200
Stop loss	0.8490
Distance between stop and target	290
Distance between stop and target / 4	72.5
Entry point (for a desired risk reward of 3:1)	0.8418 (0.8490 - 72.5)
Potential loss (risk)	72 (0.8418 - 0.8490)
Max loss trader is willing to make on trade	£200
Trade size (£ per point)	2.77 (£200/72)

Executing the trade

Coincidentally, AUD/USD is currently trading at 0.8418 to sell. So the trade is done and the stop is placed, all that's left is to monitor the position occasionally to see how it develops.

Monitoring and managing the trade

This trade would have been done around lunchtime, UK time, on the 13 August. Over the following few hours not much happens: up a bit, down a bit, but no real change. Then in the early hours of the morning the Aussie dollar nudges higher, back towards that resistance level.

Figure 5.11: example trade 2 – support and resistance

Time to panic?

Of course not. The stop is in place and so far although that resistance has been slightly breached, AUD/USD has only traded as high as 0.8478. So our trade is still intact. When the trade was placed, 0.8490 was decided on as a sensible stop loss point and that is still the case. If the market gets to that level then the original thinking behind the trade is null and void and it will be closed automatically. All of this was happening in the early hours of the morning UK time anyway, so the trader should have been oblivious to what was going on.

What should definitely *not* be done if the market approaches a stop loss, is to move that stop loss a bit further away "just in case..."

A warning on moving stops further away when the trade is in place

There are so many things wrong with doing this. It alters the risk reward of the trade and it suggests the trader has problems with admitting when a trading decision is turning out to be wrong.

It is the 'river in Egypt' approach to trading: denial (I apologise in advance for any mental stress caused by this dreadful pun).

Instead, focus on getting the stop in the right place before the trade is done. People who move stops further away while the trade is running are idiots. Let's leave it at that.

So the trade is currently under water and in danger of being stopped out. That is the nature of the game. Let's see what happened next.

Figure 5.12: example trade 2 – support and resistance

After its brief dalliance with the resistance level, the Aussie reversed sharply and over the course of the next three days proceeded to drop back to the previous low – and a little lower.

Moves like this mean (as you are constantly moving the stop *in the direction* of the trade) profit is being locked in all the time. And as the move was so steep, even if the target was not achieved by the trader, a significant portion of the points available should have been.

Next, one final example on this very simple but effective use of support and resistance. We are going to look at an even shorter-term time frame and a different currency pair.

Support and resistance – Example 3

This time we are looking at the British pound/Japanese yen exchange rate (GBP/JPY) from the third week of August 2009.

Figure 5.13: example trade 3 – support and resistance

This chart shows just over three days of trading. Each candlestick in this chart represents a 30 minute trading period during the day.

Market analysis

It can be seen that whenever GBP/JPY has weakened towards the 1.5350 area, sentiment has changed and it has rallied. The last significant rally, on 20 August, reached as high as 1.5673 before running out of steam and dropping back.

The latest 30 minute candle on the chart shows the first signs of strength creeping back in. But bear in mind this is only over the past 30 minutes. Nevertheless, this may be enough for some to think there is a trading opportunity being set up.

Let's run through the numbers as usual.

Trade planning

First the stop. The absolute low has been 1.5347, right at the beginning of the chart. So a stop below here at, say, 1.5330 seems reasonable.

Now our target. The last significant rally after the low on 19 August reached as high as 1.5673. This would seem a sensible, conservative area to aim for as a target. So we will select 1.5650 as our objective for the trade.

Once again, if we assume a risk reward entry point that gives us the potential of three times the profit versus the potential loss, the stop is subtracted from the target, resulting in a number of 320. Dividing this by four gives us a value of 80 – so adding this to the stop loss suggests an entry point of 1.5410.

With 80 points at risk on the trade and sticking to the maximum loss permitted for our particular trader of £200, then GBP/JPY should be bought at 1.5410 in the size of £2.50 per point.

Trade parameter summary

Variable	Value
Trade direction	Long
Target price for exit	1.5650
Stop loss	1.5330
Distance between stop and target	320
Distance between stop and target / 4	80
Entry point (for a desired risk reward of 3:1)	1.5410 (1.5330 + 80)
Potential loss (risk)	80
Max loss trader is willing to make on trade	£200
Trade size (£ per point)	2.50 (£200/80)

Executing the trade

At the point at which the screenshot of the chart was taken, GBP/JPY could have been bought at 1.5410. If this was missed, in the following 30 minutes it rallied past this point but then dropped back. So the trade could have been done by placing an order if the initial entry was missed.

What happened next?

Figure 5.14: example trade 3 – support and resistance

Within nine hours, 1.5650 was hit by GPB/JPY. It was quite a choppy ride up there. So if a stop was being trailed behind the market as it moved in the direction of the trade, chances are the trade would have been stopped out for a small profit around the 1.5500 level.

Maybe you would have traded it differently. But it does demonstrate, once again, how effective the idea of support and resistance can be over all sorts of time frames and various markets.

Key point:

I like this simple approach because it sets up potential low risk/high reward trades. And it gives you a definite place, based on what the market tells you, for where your stop loss should go, rather than just some random finger in the air guesstimate.

This almost wraps up the section on support and resistance. The examples I have picked so far all worked. That is the nature of examples, but do not assume that it works all the time! If markets always obeyed support and resistance levels they would just go sideways forever – and that clearly does not happen.

When support/resistance levels are broken...

The following chart shows just how explosive moves can be in forex markets (which, of course, is a big part of their appeal).

Figure 5.15: GBP/USD – breaking support/resistance

That is GBP/USD breaking what had been rock-solid support for the first half of 2008. The market moved the best part of 1800 points with only the briefest of pauses along the way. It would have been an expensive lesson in the importance of stop losses if you had bought at the support point and had no strategy for exiting if it did not go as planned...

But it is a good illustration of another basic principle of chart analysis: the importance of trends and trend following.

Which leads us neatly into the next section on trading strategy.

Trends and Trend Following

The trend is your friend.

What a well-worn cliché that is.

The trend is your friend... apart from the bend at the end.

This is a very true variation on the cliché by legendary trend-following trader Ed Seykota.

But just because it is a cliché does not make it less true. Markets *do* trend. Ignoring trends or trading against a trend can be an expensive pastime. And forex markets (maybe more so than other markets) do experience some quite impressive trends over all sorts of time frames. So it makes sense to spend some time talking about a trend-following approach to trading.

Markets can trend in three directions: up, down and sideways. No matter how much money you have, how expensive your software is, how brilliant your analysis is – we can always rely on the market moving in one of those three ways.

In the previous section, much of the movement in the markets shown was sideways, between two defined points of support and resistance. But markets do not do this all the time: we have some very clear trends in forex, across all sorts of different time frames.

Here are some examples.

Examples of trending markets in forex

USD/JPY, 1985 to 1995 – an 18,000 point slide

Figure 6.1: trending markets – USD/JPY, 1985 to 1995

EUR/GBP, October to December 2009 – a 2200 point move up

Figure 6.2: trending markets – EUR/GBP, October to December 2009

GBP/USD, part of the day 16 August 2009 – a 230 point drop

Figure 6.3: trending markets – GBP/USD, part of the day 16 August 2009

The preceding charts should illustrate well the point that trends can last from a matter of minutes to many years.

How to draw trend lines

Many technical analysts will identify a trend on the chart by using a simple trend line. This is a perfectly adequate way of tracking a trend and gauging whether it has started to run out of steam.

Over the years I have seen many weird and wacky trend lines, but as far as I am concerned there is one correct, textbook way of drawing them: they should be placed at the extreme of all the price data. So:

- in an **up trend**, the trend line goes *below* the price and

- in a **down trend** the trend line goes *above* the price.

Taking the strict approach, a trend line needs *three touches* to be considered a bona fide one. I think this is fair enough, but you have to give at least *some* leeway in what you consider a touch. Markets are seldom so obedient that they obey the textbook: obediently moving back to the trend line precisely before continuing the main trend.

The following chart gives an example of an up trend line, for GBP/USD, March to July 2009.

Figure 6.4: example of an up trend line

The following chart gives an example of a down trend line, for USD/JPY, July 3 to 8 2009.

Figure 6.5: example of a down trend line

The trend lines in both these cases clearly mark the boundaries of the trends in force. The assumption is that any move back to these lines is just a retracement of the main trend, and the main trend is expected to resume. Until, of course, it doesn't ('the bend at the end' mentioned earlier).

Trend following sits at the core of technical analysis for many people – me included. If you look at both of the previous charts, I would suggest that, once it was clear that trends were in place, it would be far less stressful to trade in the direction of these trends rather than trying to catch the short-lived moves against the trend.

As mentioned many times throughout the book: trading is not about having a crystal ball to know where prices are going to be in four days time, but playing the probabilities.

> ## Key point:
>
> Trends do not, of course, last forever, but it is a dangerous approach to try and pick a top in a major up trend, and conversely a bottom in a major down trend.

It seems perfectly sensible, if a trend is in effect, to try and ride that trend for as long as possible.

[Of course, that was a very easy sentence to type!]

The reality of doing it can be somewhat difficult: it is all too easy to spot these movements in the markets in hindsight, but we all, unfortunately, have to trade at the hard right edge of the charts – where the future is unknown.

There are many different ways of participating in a trend. But the first thing to establish is:

What time frame trend am I trying to trade?

The trend over the past five years may be up, the trend for the past two weeks may have been down, and over the past couple of days the market may have been going sideways. Which one are you trying to catch?

This is something that should be thought about before the temptation to click buy or sell is felt. You should have a clear idea of the time frame for your trade and which trend you are following, so you are not swayed by more short-term moves in the market that are probably irrelevant to the trade you have on.

What follows are a couple of examples to illustrate some techniques for trend following.

Trend following – Example 1

Our trader has decided to run a trade over days and maybe weeks and spots a clear trend in place on the US dollar/Japanese yen pair.

Figure 6.6: example 1 – USD/JPY

Market analysis

Since the 13th of the month, USD/JPY has been moving higher from the 0.9200 area and so far has reached just shy of 0.9600 before dropping back. That is a 400 point move and is the classic up trend procession of higher highs and higher lows. The market has dropped back, but held above the trend line support. (It is almost as if it was designed to be used in a book on trend-following strategies for forex.)

The idea of the trade is to follow the trend (which, for the moment, in the time frame under examination on the chart, is still up). So we know that to jump on board USD/JPY needs to be bought.

Next, as ever, the question is one of stop losses and targets.

Trade planning

Let's deal with the target first.

A conservative approach would be to look for a rally back to the last high point hit in this up trend – which was 0.9600. But I do not think it is too ambitious to expect further gains for USD/JPY based on this chart and look for the potential of a run back to those highs right from the beginning of July, before this up trend started. That would make the target 0.9690.

The next question is where should the stop go?

When it comes to trend lines one school of thought takes the view that if the trend line is broken that is it – the trend is finished. At the moment the trend line is sitting around 0.9450 so that would be one area to consider placing the stop.

But I favour a slightly different approach. The trend line *could* break and the trend can still be intact; it may just continue up at a slightly slower pace. So my preference would be to place a stop loss below the last major low on the chart. Yes it is back to that old favourite, horizontal support, for placing the stop.

The last low, identified by the horizontal line on the above chart, is at 0.9402. So a decision is made to put the stop in at 0.9390.

The stop and the target are clear. Now, it is the familiar risk reward calculation.

If USD/JPY is bought at 0.9465 then the potential profit is three times the loss. Because the stop is 75 points away, if only £200 is to be risked on this trade then the amount per point to be traded is £2.66.

Trade parameter summary

Variable	Value
Trade direction	Long
Target price for exit	0.9690
Stop loss	0.9390
Distance between stop and target	300 (0.9690 – 0.9390)
Distance between stop and target / 4	75
Entry point (for a desired risk-reward of 3:1)	0.9465 (0.9390 + 75)
Potential loss (risk)	75
Max loss trader is willing to make on trade	£200
Trade size (£ per point)	2.66 (£200/75)

The market is currently above the entry point so a bit of patience is required. An order to buy £2.66 per point at 0.9465 is placed with a stop order at 0.9390 and nothing else need be done for now.

Executing the trade

Jumping forward a few days: the order has been filled... but the trend line has been broken.

Figure 6.7: example 1 – USD/JPY

Monitoring and managing the trade

However, the market has not yet broken below the last significant low where the stop was placed. Now, even though the trend line has been broken, to me this looks like a market that is still in an up trend. The trend line break means that, admittedly, USD/JPY is not going up at the same rate as before, but there is still just about a succession of higher highs and higher lows. For my money, this trade is still valid.

What happens next is somewhat extreme...

Figure 6.8: example 1 – USD/JPY

The exit

There looks to be a news announcement that was viewed as very positive by the markets for the US dollar versus the yen and the market moved very quickly to, and beyond, the target. But this is not the important part of the chart (although it is always a nice surprise when you get a sharp two hundred point move in your favour!)

The point is that a trend was identified, a sensible stop was placed and the trade was not shaken out by the trend temporarily slackening off. The trend was followed, resulting in a nice profit compared to the risk.

Let's look at another example: this time looking to follow a down trend.

Trend following – Example 2

Figure 6.9: example 2 – EUR/USD

Market analysis

The chart shows the euro against US dollar exchange rate (EUR/USD) from late February to April 2009. Each candle represents one day of trading. It can be seen that EUR/USD has been in decline since the third week of March, moving down from the 1.3700 area to as low as 1.2900. Over the last nine days or so it has rallied back to the down trend line, and also the previous significant high which was at 1.3392.

Trade planning

Assuming this down trend from March is going to continue, it seems reasonable enough to go short here with a stop loss above that recent high. So 1.3415 will be the stop loss on the trade.

When it comes to the target for the trade, a run back to the April lows would be a conservative one, with the early March lows around 1.2500 a more ambitious one. Let's go for the big move and choose 1.2500 as the target.

If a three to one risk reward is required, it means the trade needs to go on at 1.3187. But at the moment the market is trading at 1.3230 to sell – if the trade is done at this level the potential risk versus reward is going to be even bigger than three to one.

The remaining calculation is the position sizing. Selling short at 1.3230 and using a stop loss of 1.3415 means the potential risk in points is 185, which translates into a pound per point trade of £1.08, assuming a risk of £200 is satisfactory.

Trade parameter summary

Variable	Value
Trade direction	Short
Target price for exit	1.2500
Stop loss	1.3415
Distance between stop and target	915 (1.3415 - 1.2500)
Distance between stop and target / 4	229
Entry point (for a desired risk-reward of 3:1)	1.3187 (1.3415 - 229)
Actual entry point	1.3230
Potential loss (risk)	185
Max loss trader is willing to make on trade	£200
Trade size (£ per point)	1.08 (£200/185)

Executing the trade

So the trade is done: EUR/USD is sold short at 1.3230 at £1.08 per point.

Figure 6.10: example 2 – EUR/USD

The exit

Three days later. EUR/USD moves higher, through the 1.3400 level and the trade is stopped out for a loss. The reasoning behind the trade was valid, but you can't win them all. Taking manageable losses is part and parcel of trading any financial market.

This wraps up the section on identifying and trading with trends. There are many examples that could be looked at here but I think these two examples illustrate the principles perfectly.

It is time to get onto the next topic (and if you could fill a whole book with examples of support, resistance and trend following, then you could fill a library on the next topic: trading using indicators).

Indicators – A More Mathematical
Approach to Trading

If there has been one growth area in technical analysis over recent years, then indicators is it. As more people have become interested in charting, and computers and clever software have proliferated, the number of indicators seems to increase every year.

It can be very confusing to the new trader:

Should I use RSI, stochastic or MACD?

Is a ten period Bollinger Band better than a three day Directional Movement Index?

Will a parabolic stop-and-reverse system make me more attractive to the opposite sex?

It's a minefield out there.

The danger is that all these different indicators encourage new practitioners to believe that there is a Holy Grail system out there. A system that is right all the time.

If only I can get the settings on my Chaikin indicator correct, all my trading problems will disappear...

It is not surprising that the charts of new traders can end up looking something like the following.

Figure 7.1: Example chart

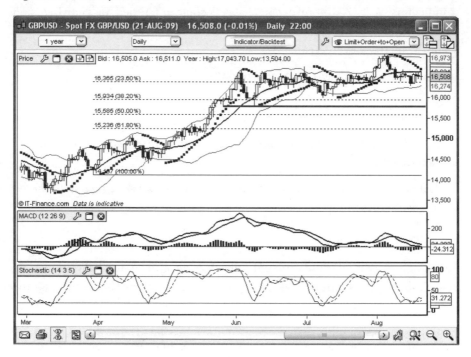

As a study in contemporary modern art it may be something you would be happy to have hanging on your wall, but I would question the usefulness of having so many different indicators on a chart.

The objective of course is to make money, and if it works for you, more power to your elbow. But for many of us, throwing so much stuff at a price chart can result in 'analysis paralysis'. Half of it says buy, half of it says sell and you end up losing focus on the big picture, such as what the price is actually doing.

> As a beginner myself, I can remember many a wasted evening in the mid-1990s tweaking my stochastics, in search of the perfect never-lose system. I am sure I would be still searching for the perfect combination today if I had kept at it.

I am not anti indicators, but I do think their importance is over emphasised.

Indicators definitely have their place But for me it is as part of an overall strategy, and not the be all and end all of trading.

For this section we are going to take a look at one of the most basic (as usual, I am in favour of keeping it simple): the Relative Strength Index.

Relative Strength Index (RSI)

RSI was developed in the late 1970s by J. Welles Wilder, and as such is one of the oldest mathematical indicators for technical analysis. It compares the historical gains for a market over a certain period, with its losses over the same period. The RSI value is bounded by zero and 100.

The calculation looks like this:

```
RSI = 100 -    100
            _____
             1 + RS

where,

RS = Average Gain/Average Loss
```

When developing the indicator, Welles Wilder used a period of 14 days. So RS is the average daily change for those days (out of the last 14) when the market rose, divided by the average daily change for those days (out of the last 14) when the market fell.

When the average gain is more than the average loss, then the RSI will rise (because RS will be greater than one – and vice versa).

To take a very simple (but unlikely) example, if one decided to calculate RSI with a period of 2 days, and for the previous two days the market performance had been:

```
Day 1: +30%
Day 2: -10%
```

then RS would be calculated as (30/10), and the RSI would be 75.

Before we look at the charts for RSI, let's deal with something that is sometimes a contentious issue: the number of periods used for the RSI.

Deciding what period to use

Welles Wilder chose 14 for his formula, but you can use any value you want. Which leads us to a problem with indicators: the extent to which they can be tweaked.

I am sure much computing power has been expended over the past few years in the pursuit of the perfect period value. But I don't think there is an answer to this. Whenever I use RSI on a daily chart I always use a value of ten (as that covers the previous two trading weeks). Please do not think this is the perfect number (you are free to use whatever you want), but that is the unscientific reason for the value used by me in the examples in this book.

Let's see what this indicator looks like on the chart.

Figure 7.2: RSI, GBP/USD

The chart shown is GBP/USD for January to August 2009. The squiggly line at the bottom of the chart is the 10 day RSI. You should be able to see straightaway why the RSI is referred to as an oscillator – because it oscillates between two boundaries (zero and 100).

You can see from the chart how the RSI value changes over time as the market moves around. The standard analysis of RSI holds that:

- a value **below 30** signals an *oversold* situation for the market, the market has fallen too far, too fast and is due a bounce; while

- a value **above 70** signals the market is *overbought*, the market has rallied too far too fast and is due a slide.

Most software will draw horizontal lines on the RSI to signal the 30 and 70 bands (these are shown on the chart above).

Let's look at the first few months of 2009 a bit more closely.

Figure 7.3: RSI, GBP/USD

The GBP/USD rate slid in late January – it actually fell to its lowest point in more than 20 years. Correspondingly the RSI also fell, dipping below the 30 mark, suggesting that the market was oversold and due at least a small rally. After a few days the market did bounce back and the RSI turned higher, peaking in the first half of February before starting to tail off again and approach the oversold area in early March (the lowest level reached here was 31).

Then GBP/USD starts to recover once more, dragging the RSI back up with it. The RSI reached as high as 73 in late March – which coincides with the peak of GBP/USD for that particular rally. The RSI is giving an overbought signal, and GBP/USD dutifully drops more than 600 points over the next five days.

Isn't that fantastic!

This looks like a great system. (The money that this book cost you can now be repaid many times over!) But market conditions have favoured the RSI here.

> ## Key point:
>
> Oscillators tend to perform at their best when markets are trading sideways.

It is true that in this period the RSI performed reasonably well. A trading strategy that followed the signals given looks like it would have been a profitable one. But these sorts of indicators tend to perform better when markets are trading in a sideways fashion. When a market suddenly starts trending, it can get very ugly, very quickly for the RSI.

We will jump forward and have a look at what GBP/USD was up to at the beginning of May.

Figure 7.4: GBP/USD – April–May 2009

It can be seen that GBP/USD has spent the past couple of months gradually rising. It has gained more than 1400 points in the period shown in this chart, going from 1.3600 through 1.5000. The RSI has not done a bad job of calling the temporary tops along the way. And the RSI has now gone into the overbought zone.

Now, having read the previous strategy section, you should be aware there is a clear trend in place – and it is up. It can be very dangerous to trade against the trend, but if you were putting blind faith in the ability of the RSI to predict the market you would now be going short GBP/USD.

Let's look at how events unfolded.

Figure 7.5: GBP/USD – April–May 2009

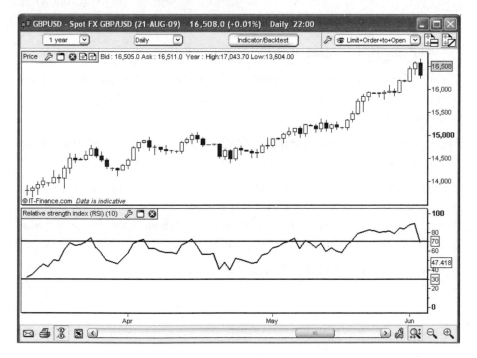

Nasty.

Unfortunately, GBP/USD rather inconsiderately did not realise it was meant to drop. It continued to rise, gaining almost 1500 points over the course of the next few weeks before experiencing any hint of weakness.

Key point:

This is an extreme example but it does demonstrate, yet again, why it is important to have a strategy for getting out if things do not work as planned.

This does not mean the RSI has no value. Used as part of an overall strategy it can highlight opportunities and help stack the odds in your favour and can complement other approaches such as support, resistance and trend following.

A twist on RSI – spotting divergences

There is another way of using oscillators such as the RSI, one which many people consider to be a more effective approach than simply looking for overbought/oversold situations.

These signals are rarer but are thought to be more reliable. It concerns looking for *divergences* between how the price and RSI are moving.

If the market is trending up, the RSI should be following suit, and vice versa. It is when the price is doing one thing and the RSI something else that divergence happens. And it can give a hint, for example, that the trend that is in effect for the price may be running out of steam.

Here is an example on EUR/USD from early 2009.

Figure 7.6: RSI bullish divergence, EUR/USD

In the early part of the chart, EUR/USD was edging lower and the RSI was following suit. The euro hit a low versus the dollar in mid-February, and the RSI moved into oversold territory. EUR/USD then bounced before turning back down into March and setting a fresh low for this particular move.

But – and this is the divergence signal – the RSI has started to trend higher, because it has made a higher low above the oversold zone.

This is called *bullish divergence* – a suggestion that the trend you are following on price, may be at risk of running and out of steam and at least partially reversing.

The flipside of bullish divergence is *bearish divergence*, which can be seen in the following chart.

Figure 7.7: RSI bearing divergence, EUR/USD

It is not quite as textbook, or pretty, an example as the first one but in the real world we often have to deal with less than perfect situations.

EUR/USD has been pushing steadily higher, but as it moves to a fresh high for this particular move, the RSI seems to have lost interest and is making a lower high, rather than following the market higher.

Again, a clue that the trend may be running out of steam.

Rare – and worth taking note of

As I said, divergence is a rarer signal than the straightforward overbought/oversold set ups. For me, because it is less common, it is worth paying attention to.

Ideally, I would want to use it near a definite area of support and resistance so there is a clear point for a stop loss to go.

A more aggressive approach would be to follow the divergence signal, but exit as soon as the market continued its trend, making the signal clearly invalid. In the above example that would mean going short when the divergence signal appeared, but with a stop loss just above the most recent high in this particular up trend for the price. If EUR/USD continued higher after the divergence, then the trend clearly is not running out of steam and the divergence has failed.

Oscillators can add an extra dimension to your trading decisions and if you understand how to interpret one, such as the RSI covered here, similar techniques can be applied to other oscillators such as stochastics and MACD.

...And Finally

Phew, the end. After doing all that writing I am completely forex-ed out.

This book was written with both the novice and more experienced spread better in mind and I do hope that the explanations, principles and strategies in it are useful for your trading.

For those of you yet to start spread betting or, more specifically, start spread betting forex, I have one piece of advice:

Start!

I have met far too many people over the years who are about to start spread betting... just as soon as they have found the perfect system... or made more time... or got their charting set-up just right... or attended a few more seminars. There is always a reason not to start. If I bump into these people again a few months later they are usually still nearly, almost ready. Yes... definitely... starting next month.

Like so many things in life, you can only learn so much from thinking, watching and reading about the subject. With the minimum trading sizes at many spread betting companies now so low you can start trading at a much lower level than ever before – so you can dip your toe in, try out the strategies and not risk losing your shirt.

For those of you already active, I hope the book has added something to your trading – whether that is identifying some potential new strategies, or variations on what you use already, or to give more thought to the importance of risk. As I mentioned in the risk chapter, this is the area that over the years I have seen too many people give scant regard to – with predictably painful results for their account. If my book means that more people are mindful of placing stop losses (in the right places) and trading at a sensible size relative to the size of their account, then I think that is a job well done.

The best bit of advice I ever received was to keep records of my trades and results. If you are trading off charts, print out a copy of the chart and make some basic notes on why you made the trade and file it away. I did this for years and it is surprising when I go back and review the charts how many – on reflection, away from the screen – actually looked to be just fifty-fifty trades. There is a strong temptation for all of us to see what we want to as an excuse for doing something.

> ## Key point:
>
> Learning to recognise the situations when there really is not a sensible trade is an important part of honing a successful strategy.

...and finally, finally

For all of us there is no end point when it comes to trading. We all learn more as we go along. I hope this book helped you along the learning process a little bit.

Index